M000086408

WALKING ON WATER

TRUSTING GOD
WITH THE IMPOSSIBLE

RAYMOND FRIZZELLE

Unless otherwise noted, all Scripture taken from the New King James Version®. Copyright © 1982 by Thomas Nelson. Used by permission.

Walking on Water:

Trusting God With the Impossible

Copyright © 2019 by Raymond Frizelle

ISBN-978-1677747016

Layout Design: Glory Publishing Services

Cover Design: Christian Ophus

All rights reserved. No part of this publication may be reproduced, distributed, or transmitted in any form or by any means, including photocopying, recording, or other electronic or mechanical methods, without the prior written permission of the publisher, except in the case of brief quotations embodied in critical reviews and certain other noncommercial uses permitted by copyright law.

DEDICATION

This book is dedicated to Jesus Christ, the author and finisher of our faith and the one who provides every miracle. We give Him all the glory and praise for every miracle (past, present and future).

This book is also dedicated to my precious wife, Cynthia, who has prayed and stood beside me on this journey. The gifts God has placed in her life have brought balance to our journey in ministry. She has been the joy of my life as we have experienced God's miracle power. Her passion for God and others has touched the lives of so many people. Also, we are grateful for our precious children, Melissa and Doug, and Aaron and Regan, and our grandchildren who have blessed our lives by following Jesus Christ.

We dedicate this story of miracles to the many, many prayer warriors God has sent into our lives. Only Heaven will know all God has allowed in this journey.

ENDORSEMENTS

Walking on a Water is a powerful testament to the miraculous power of God in lives today! Miracles were not just for Biblical times and this book proves that, once again. Legacy (what we leave to our families and generations to come) is so important. God instructed Moses to have the stories of God's deliverance "told to their children's children," in order to preserve their heritage. It's vital that we carry on that tradition for maximum impact of "Who we Are and What we Believe." We highly recommend this book for inspiration to anyone who needs the encouragement to believe and know that God is able to move any mountain!

Mark and Susie Purkey
Evangelists

I cried tears for the heartbreaks and cried tears rejoicing over the wondrous miracles! We serve an amazing God!! I am very happy to give my endorsement of this wonderful book, *Walking on Water*. In Christ,

Martha Jordan
Writer/Author

I love this book and was captivated from the start. As you turn the pages, you'll feel as if you've been invited into the home of someone whose greatest joy is knowing the Lord. The personal stories are a reminder that "the way out is through"… through trust in God and His Word. If I were to describe my brother, Raymond, in one word, it would be peacemaker. He is a humble individual who always seeks to lift others up and turn their eyes to Jesus and His Word. I've seen him step out on the water many times to follow the leading of God. I've also seen him stay faithful to his calling during difficult seasons when others might have quit. Thanks to the wonderful example that our parents set, we grew up knowing God as our Savior, Friend, Counselor, and Miracle Maker. Out of hardships, we experienced many miracles, big and small. This training ground prepared Raymond to answer the call to the ministry and continue a life-long journey of "walking on water" with Jesus. If you're in need of a miracle or just want to trust God with more of your life than you ever have before, this book, *Walking on Water*, is for you.

Elizabeth (Frizzelle) Burgoyne

If there are singular words that would describe the legacy of the Frizzelle family, they would be 'obedience' and 'miraculous'. *Walking on Water* reveals a family committed to obeying their Lord when he says, "get out of the boat and come", just as Peter did when he experienced the miracle of walking on water. Because of unwavering obedience and the goodness of God, this family has experienced the miraculous time and time again. Get ready to have your faith inspired as you read this book.

Jim and Pam King
Pastors/Evangelists

It is one thing to read stories about miracles from a book, but it is a whole new perspective to actually be a part of them. Raymond and Cynthia, whom I also call Dad and Mom, have always taught us that there is a "miracle in motion" if we just take time to let God show up. They have experienced miracles and have also been the instruments in other people's lives where there were miracles. I cannot deny God's reality and presence in my life when I look over the years and see all the things that some would call luck, karma or just good timing. I cannot call them anything less than a miracle. Don't just read this book, *Walking on Water*, live this truth--that with God ALL things are possible.

Aaron Frizzelle
West Campus Pastor/Hope Fellowship, Frisco, TX

Raymond and Cynthia Frizzelle are two of the most genuine ordinary people I know that have grasped the meaning of living life in the extraordinary, trusting our living God with the impossible! Knowing Christ in us is the substance that produces the reality of trusting God with the impossible. *Walking on Water* presents Jesus alive, in the ordinary life with convincing proof, as well as challenges believers to raise expectations to live the God-life, fully immersed in the extraordinary. Unlock the extraordinary life you're meant to live in life's journey... read *Walking on Water*.

Huey P. Long
Evangelist/Missionary/Pastor/City Manager

As we read *Walking On Water*, we recalled many of the miracles that were recounted. Pastor Frizzelle has been our Pastor for over 17 years and we have watched him and his wife, Cynthia, minister tirelessly as they demonstrate God's Grace not only to the church body but to the community and city. He gives God all the glory and credit for each miracle. We pray God's blessing over this book and the Frizzelles' ministry.

Darrell and Kathey Wyrick
Church Leadership

When I received a draft copy of this book of God's miracle working power in the lives of Raymond and Cynthia Frizzelle and testimonies from some of our church family, I sat and read the entire copy before retiring that evening. I have been a part of our church family for more than 55 years and the anecdotal histories of people you will read in this book are well known to me. Seldom do we meet without someone being reminded of how they have been personally blessed when hearing of or having been the subject of God's miracle power. Many have been verified by medical doctors and all are verified by our daily witness and the lives of these people receiving miracles. It is a personal privilege to recommend *Walking on Water* to you.

Alan Barnes
Miami Integris Hospital Chaplain/Church Leadership

The Frizzelles' lives have been filled with miracles. Anyone who reads **Walking On Water** will have reassurance that our God is a miracle working God. We feel very blessed that we were asked to share our miracles in this book as witnesses to this miracle working God.

Charles and Barbara Stoner
Miracle Recipients/Church Leadership

Miracles for the Frizzelle family are not just a life occurrence, but they are a way of life. I have always, since my earliest remembrance, been very aware of the goodness of God to miraculously bring change to our circumstances, even when there seemingly was absolutely no way out. There's a favorite Frizzelle saying, "There's a miracle in the making"…and we have seen one right after the other. I personally have watched God touch Pastor Raymond and Cynthia and their entire family with miracles that no one could logically explain. I believe this book will sovereignly challenge you to go beyond any experience you've ever had and step up into the most miraculous season of your life… one you will powerfully realize is yours to possess and expect from your Heavenly Father. May you be wonderfully blessed as you read **Walking on Water**.

Clyde Frizzelle

Walking on Water will touch and encourage anyone who reads it as well as uplift their faith to believe for the impossible. The Frizzelles have experienced multiple miracles throughout their lives, whether it was needing an emotional healing from losing someone in death, needing finances to fulfill the call of God on their lives or healing them physically, God never let them down. In a world that needs to see God is alive and supernatural, start looking for the chance to give God the opportunity to show how big of a God He is.

Ron Rhoads
Evangelist, Founder/International Soccer Salvation Camps & Crusades Ministry Mount Joy, PA

Walking on Water will strengthen your faith to believe in miracles. When you are in the middle of the making of a miracle it's hard to see on the other side, but this is the opportunity for Jesus to step in. It allows us to see that He is our source, when all of our sources and options have run out. I'm so grateful I grew up in a family that not only walked through so many miracles, but prays for them and shares them with others. It brings so much hope and encouragement. The enemy wants to make us feel isolated and like we are the only ones walking through struggles, but when we share our testimony it brings it into the light and creates hope for others.

Melissa (Frizzelle) Young

As you read *Walking on Water* your faith will be encouraged and you will learn God still gives miracles today. Pastor Frizzelle and his family found themselves in many desperate situations throughout their lives, but they knew and believed, and with their foundation in the Bible, their faith and trust in God and in asking His will, the answers would come. The only question was when and how He would answer their prayers. The testimonies of miracles in the congregation of Miami First Assembly also help to uplift and build faith in God's miracles.

One doesn't need to read a book
On how to pastor well
Simply follow the footsteps of
Pastor Raymond and Cynthia Frizzelle.

Bill and Joy Stoner
Miracle Recipients/Church Leadership

Walking On Water--the name says it all..."WOW". Many miracles are recounted in this book, and faith "downloads" with each one. Find your favorite, let your faith arise and listen for your name to be called..."get out of the boat and come"...then add your miracle story.

Darrell and Paula Vanpool
Miracle recipients/Church-Prayer Leadership

FOREWORD

Do you believe in miracles? Have you ever experienced a miracle? Do you have a need for a miracle in your life? Do you want to know more about miracles...even read some true stories about real miracles that really did happen...to ordinary people...miracles that are even documented? Page by page in this book, *Walking on Water*, Raymond Frizzelle recounts "adventures in miracles", not only in his life and the lives of his family, but testimonies of miracles from members of his church congregation. Settings for the miracles are carefully noted as are the needs for the respective miracles. Expectations for the climax of each miracle keep the reader in suspense of "what's next". The Holy Spirit provides the anointing over each miracle story, and quickly the reader will be "on site", anxiously awaiting conclusion of one miracle, and ready for the next one. Maybe, as in my case, you will find yourself often on "holy ground", caught up in the awe and glory of the moment, humbled in the presence of the Trinity.

Miracles are not a foreign "happening" to Raymond Frizzelle. His life is made up of miracles...some bigger than others, but not one that does not give testimony to the presence of God in his life, and not one for which he does not give the glory to God. He is a man of God, strongly devoted in his beliefs and Christian witness, and desire to share the salvation message of God's word with any and every one he meets. This is the man who had a dream to write a book about the miracles of God he and his family have experienced over the years. This is the book that recounts many of those miracles and through which he shares belief that miracles are just waiting to happen…in the lives of his family, in the flock he shepherds, and…in yours. I am one of many sheep in his flock. I have witnessed his faith in action and experienced the sincerity and power of his prayers.

Raymond Frizzelle and his wife, Cynthia, have been in ministry at Miami First Assembly since February 2003. They came to Miami "mission minded", soul-winning focused, and miracle believing people. Their own stories of their experiences in these areas of ministry are fascinating. They are two humble people who take God's word for truth, apply it to life, and seek to find ministry opportunity, day by day, year by year, always giving glory to God…ALWAYS!

Welcome to the reading of *Walking on Water*. May God's presence accompany you as you read each chapter…and along the way, somewhere, I pray your grain of mustard seed will be nurtured and you find the path to gaining your miracle.

Paula Vanpool (Miracle Recipient)
Retired Educator/Consultant/Writer

PREFACE

Come, he said. Then Peter got down out of the boat,
walked on the water and came toward Jesus.

MATTHEW 14:29 (NKJV)

Experiencing the miracle working power of God is such a wonderful blessing and something never to be forgotten. Most of us love to hear of miracles that have taken place in others' lives, but when a miracle takes place in one's own life, it marks that place and will be remembered, always. The rest of the story is in the desperation of having no answer but God to meet the crisis. As God leads you through each situation, your faith will grow and you will begin to expect miracles.

Nothing states it better than the Word of God:

Now faith is the substance of things hoped for,
the evidence of things not seen.

HEBREWS 11:1 (NKJV)

Many times, Cynthia and I have seen and felt the miracle by faith, long before it happened. Other times, only long after the miracle occurred, did we recognize it and understand God's way.

ACKNOWLEDGEMENTS

For with God nothing will be impossible.
Luke 1:37 (NKJV)

Thank you to all those who have stood with us through the years of our miracles, birthed by desperation for God's intervention and supernatural power. A special thank you to Cynthia, my precious wife, who has stood by my side in every trial and victory; in every crisis, our precious children and family have experienced the power of God. Many prayer warriors have held up our hands through many years of serving God and ministry opportunities. We pray you will be encouraged to believe God for the impossible as you read through this book.

Thank you to Sue Williams for her many hours of work dedicated to converting our original hand-written script to typed script. Thank you to our daughter-in-law, Regan, for doing the first journalist edit of our original typed script for the book. A special thank you to Paula Vanpool for the untold hours spent in the massive task of consulting with Cynthia and me in the writing, editing and proofing of this book.

ACKNOWLEDGEMENTS

Thank you to those who provided written testimonies of miracles that are included in this book. To both Darrell and Paula Vanpool, thank you for your endless hours of prayer work and support of our lives and ministry.

To Mr. Richard Exley, Mr. Jim Miller, Ms. Martha Jordan and Ms. Julie Werner...thank you for your help in making this dream of our book become a reality.

Pastor Raymond Frizzelle

CONTENTS

INTRODUCTION:
Seed Beds
of a Miracle

Seek the Lord while He may be found,
Call *upon Him while He is near.*

ISAIAH 55:6 (NKJV)

A s we take this journey (walking on water), it is important to give all the glory to God and know He is no respecter of persons. What He has done for my family and me, He will do for you. Every story we have walked through, God has proven faithful. God has many ways He answers prayer and your miracle is just ahead as you ask and believe in this supernatural God.

A miracle is effectively defined in Google's definition as "a surprising and welcome event that is not explained by natural or scientific laws and therefore considered to be the work of a divine agency." (I will define the divine agency for you…God).

In understanding a miracle, let me describe it as a place of desperation or need in which only God's intervention, wisdom and supernatural power can bring resolution (solve). You need a miracle when facing something that is seemingly IMPOSSIBLE.

Matthew 14:22-33 is the account of Peter walking on water to Jesus and his experience of the miracle that Jesus led him through. First, Jesus had sent the disciples ahead to cross the Sea of Galilee, knowing they would encounter a storm. At the moment of their need, He came to them, walking on the water in the middle of the storm. They cried out to Him in their fear and Jesus spoke comfort. It was then that Peter asked this question, " Lord, if it is You, command me to come to You on the water." Jesus said "Come." It was then that Peter came out of the boat and walked on water. It would have been easier for Peter to have stayed in the boat, but he was not afraid to ask, and Jesus said, "Yes."

Peter experienced the impossible, while the rest watched. Yes, he looked at the storm and began to sink, but Jesus reached out and pulled him up and the storm ceased. That's experiencing the supernatural miracle working power of God by stepping out of the boat and letting faith get you to Jesus.

You will read of many miracles, but the greatest miracle is the day you meet Jesus as your personal Savior and encounter a good God. Our heavenly Father sent His only son, Jesus Christ, that you might have life and have it more abundantly. The Holy Spirit encourages us to receive the Power of God in every circumstance of life. Let your faith arise and get ready for a miracle.

CHAPTER 1*
Our Beginnings... from Miracles

*For as the body without the spirit is dead,
so faith without works is dead also.*
JAMES 2:26 (NKJV)

J esus spoke to the ten lepers in the village who saw Him and (**asked**) for His mercy to be on them, telling them to go show themselves to the priest (Luke 17:14). Scripture says as they went (**obeyed**) they were cleansed (**healed**)... but only one of the lepers who saw he was healed turned back to (**give God the glory**). Miracles take steps of faith (sometimes including doctors' hands) as the miracles are received. That's faith and works combined for the miracles. *Giving God glory* is the ultimate of our works (obedience).

Several things have shaped the lives Cynthia and I have lived in experiencing God's miracles in our own lives as well as in lives in our family. (I met Cynthia Clements at Gospel Lighthouse Church; I was twenty-two and she was eighteen when we married.) Our mothers and grandmothers experienced the pain of divorce, some more than once, and we determined that, with God's help, we would break the cycle of divorce in our generation. Both of our families experienced passion for God and the power of the full gospel message. (Research on my father's side of our family confirms the Nicks family was part of the "Great Revival" in Kentucky and Tennessee in the early 1800s. Absalom Doak Nicks, Jr. was born in 1826 and was a blacksmith by trade and a Church of Christ preacher. It was said that while working at his forge he always kept a Bible at hand to read as he worked. He also served as a State Representative during the administration of Andrew Jackson.) This passion has continued in our family, as you will see in the true stories that are recounted in this book. Cynthia and I purposed that, with God's help, we would walk in faith and power of the Holy Spirit. We love people and have experienced miracles, not only in our lives, but have witnessed them in the churches where we have served through our years of ministry in Kingdom work.

My Beginning

I was born March 30, 1954, in Fort Worth, Texas, to Clyde and Delores Frizzelle. I had the "miracle" privilege of being born into a Christian family that took the whole word of God as past, present and eternal truth. My parents had five children (four sons, one daughter); I am number two in the lineup.

My father came from a good family with a Church of Christ background, but they really did not have personal relationships with Jesus

Christ. There were thirteen children in the family (twelve boys and one girl). He was number twelve in the lineup. His father died when he was eight years old. He quit school in the eighth grade to help support his family. He served in WWII in Germany from May 24, 1944, to June 20, 1946. At twenty-nine, unsaved, he met and married my mother.

My mother came from a very dysfunctional family. Her mother was married and divorced five times. Her grandmother was the godly person in her life. She took her to church, prayed for her, and invested in her young life. When my mother was ten years old, her grandmother died, leaving her nurtured with prayers and "seeds planted". She and her brother would walk to church as she had done with her grandmother. Completing school through the tenth grade, she married young and ended up in an abusive marriage and divorce, losing her first son to pneumonia during that marriage. Seeking God in the prime of the mess in her life, she began attending Southside Assembly of God Church in Fort Worth, Texas. There she met a dear sister in Christ who became the influence as her "new spiritual grandmother" and prayer partner. With encouragement from this "spiritual grandmother" and her pastor, she chose to attend Southwestern Assemblies of God College in Waxahachie, Texas, and to study to follow God. It was there in a prayer room that she cried out to God in her desperateness and God spoke to her heart that He was going to give her four sons who would be involved in ministry. At age twenty she met and married my father.

My father experienced salvation at Northside Assembly of God in Ft. Worth. Shortly after salvation, he was filled with the baptism of the Holy Spirit. His birth family turned away from him when he got involved with a Pentecostal Church (Assemblies of God). When I was in the third grade, he was called into evangelistic work. Our home church experienced five years of weekly revivals and we spent most of our evenings in church. My dad became an avid student of the Word, especially the book of Revelations. He was never in full time ministry, but worked at Bell Helicopter to support his family until his death (invented two major tools for them while working for them). He ended up ministering to many of his siblings and did many of their funerals. At the age of forty-four, he had a heart attack and died in the hospital. Later he told us, during those moments of death, he had gone through the heavens and had seen Jesus. Jesus asked him if he wanted to come home or return to earth with his family. He asked if he could return home until his children (my parents had those four sons, and one daughter) were grown and that when the Lord was ready for him, would he just please come and take him home without him having to return to the hospital? He came back to life (a miracle) and lived until his children were grown. (I have served in full time ministry for over thirty years. My three brothers and sister have all, at some time in their lives, served in the ministry.) In January 1985, just a few months before my thirty-first birthday, God called him home on a Saturday night, with no pain or trauma, just one final breath and then heaven. God granted his request.

In 1997, while on staff at Lawton First Assembly of God in Lawton, Oklahoma, I was ordained in Oklahoma City at our District office. I remain in full time ministry and am so thankful for the years of my father's presence in my life, and the memories of his time in ministry and his love of God's word.

Cynthia's Beginning

Blessed is the man who trusts in the Lord,
And whose hope is the Lord.
JEREMIAH 17:7 (NKJV)

Cynthia was born May 4, 1958, in Dallas, Texas, to John and Betty Jean (Jeanne) Clements She was their third child, second daughter. Her mother miscarried the oldest child, a son. They experienced great difficulty as a family and her parents divorced when Cynthia was only two years old.

Cynthia's mother was the youngest of seven children born to Cynthia's Grandmother, Annie Chapman (a beautiful full-blooded Cherokee Indian). Annie's first husband died a short time after they married; they had no children. Her second husband was killed while working on the railroad, leaving her with two sons and two daughters. The mother of four children, she married a third time, with hope of having help in raising her children. During this marriage, both Annie and their infant daughter were hospitalized with influenza. Annie survived, but their baby daughter died. She then had a third son and a fourth daughter, Cynthia's mother, the youngest by eight years from her brother. Jeanne never knew her father. He was unfaithful to her mother, and after she was born, Annie was left to raise her two youngest children, as well as keep relationships with her four older children, all of whom were grown. Annie gave full attention to Jeanne in caring for her and all their small family needs, leaving her youngest child with little responsibility, which left her with lots of time for herself. Annie became a Christian when her second born son came home from WWII. He was in the Army group that landed and attacked at Normandy on "D-Day". All of his group died during their attack and he alone survived. It was at that moment, in a fox hole, he cried out to God for salvation and made a promise to witness to his family when he returned. He kept his

7

promise and Cynthia's family found Jesus as Savior, one by one. Annie attended Gospel Lighthouse and remained a devoted Christian and prayer warrior the rest of her life. She was the major Christian influence in Cynthia's life.

Cynthia's father, John, was one of three children born to Edward and Thelma Clements. They were very poor and John's mother left his dad and her small children to venture out into life, making her living as a prostitute. They never saw her again until later in life. Hoping to have help raising his children, Edward married again. From this marriage, he had two more sons. John and his sisters were not taken care of as his dad had hoped they would be. His step-mother was abusive to her three step-children, taking interest only in the two sons she had given birth to. At twelve years old, John ran away, and was housed in a youth detention facility for a while. By seventeen, John was on his own. He met Cynthia's mother (two years younger than he was) and at age fifteen she miscarried their first child. Cynthia's mother dropped out of school and they married. By eighteen, he had joined the service.

He also served in Germany during WWII. At age eighteen, Jeanne had their second child, a daughter. Twenty-one months later, they had their third child, Cynthia. Her father provided for his family, taking jobs wherever he could find work. To make sure they were taken care of during his absence when working away from them, he moved his wife and two daughters in with his step-mother, (Mamaw). They were a dysfunctional family of four, and when Cynthia was two years old, her parents divorced and her mother moved into an apartment with her two daughters. Hoping she had found someone to take care of her and her two small daughters, Jeanne soon remarried. Cynthia's dad later remarried and adopted his two step-children. Cynthia and her sister did not see him often. It was not until the last year of his life that he and Cynthia reconciled, and she finally experienced the love and approval of her father.

Thinking she had married an older man of God who would take care of them, Cynthia's mother would take her and her sister to where he preached at a mission's house (precursor to an AA/halfway house type of program), but soon realized he was not what he appeared to be. For two years Cynthia, her sister and mother, lived at the mercy of an abusive alcoholic step-father/husband, often fearful for their lives. Cynthia's mother was able to escape with her two small daughters, and divorced her second husband. She returned home to her mother, Annie, with her two daughters. She remarried in October 1975 (eight months before Cynthia and I married) and they have continued to celebrate that anniversary every year since.

Cynthia and her sister lived in Dallas, Texas, with their mother and grandmother, Annie, in the small house on Exeter Street that Annie called home. They attended church with Annie at Gospel Lighthouse. Annie took care of the girls while Cynthia's mother worked and attended to caring for herself. Annie taught them to cook (delicious peach cobbler that Cynthia still makes to this day), keep house, and many other things to prepare them to care for their own homes and families one day.

Granny Chapman's Peach Cobbler

Dough--2 cups flour/1 cup Crisco shortening/dash of salt/ water to moisten and roll out

Filling--peaches-3 cups sliced/sugar-1 1/2 cups/butter-1/2 cup/water-1/4 cup mixed with 2-3 tablespoons flour/Mexican vanilla-dash

Simmer peach mixture to thicken; roll out half of dough for base in glass pan; pour in peach mixture and cover with lattice dough; top with cinnamon, butter and oats; then bake at 350 degrees until bubbly

Cynthia and her sister shared the one bedroom in that small house with their mother and grandmother. Cynthia's precious grandmother prayed over her nightly and told her that there were things she herself was too shy to do for the Lord (speak in tongues/give interpretation, pray for/love people and more), but that she, Cynthia, would do those things one day. Cynthia gave her heart to Jesus at age six and was filled with the Baptism of the Holy Spirit at age twelve, while praying for her cousin. She loved going to church with her "Granny" and learning about the Lord and praying. When Cynthia was twelve years old, her Granny died and Cynthia went into a deep depression. She loved her grandmother dearly and did not think she could live without her presence in her life. Granny meant everything to Cynthia, and at her death, she felt she had lost everything.

The great grief that Cynthia experienced with the death of her grandmother manifested in physical symptoms. She had migraine headaches, blackouts and other issues associated with her grief over the absence of her grandmother in her life. When taken to the doctor, she was given valium to help her deal with her grief and depression. Cynthia chose not to take that or any other medication, believing the Lord would help her. The Lord confirmed this to her very soon. In a church service she attended, her pastor spoke to those in attendance, stating that there was someone who was dealing with some issues, and not to take the medication that the doctor had prescribed. Having this confirmed to her, she went home and flushed the entire number of pills out of her life. The depression lifted, and she gained her freedom...she had experienced a miracle. She continued to grow in the Lord, still living with her sister and mother in Dallas, attending Gospel Lighthouse Church.

In 1974 Cynthia and her mother were driving in Oak Cliff, Texas, running usual Saturday errands. They were in their black and white Rambler. Recounting the story, Cynthia remembers that car well. From the day they bought it, it had a leak in the window or air vent and when it rained water would pour onto the floor board. The mats had been removed and when it rained, Cynthia's mother would put an old towel down to soak up the water while they kept their feet high so not to get wet. They had little money, but did the best they could as the floor rusted more and more with each rain. On that day of running errands, Cynthia's mother stepped on the clutch, and as she did, it fell through the car floor board onto the street. As she began crying and wondering what to do, a kind man from the gas station and garage across the street came over to help them. He got in the car and pushed it with his foot to move it across the street into his station. He offered Cynthia's mother $100 for the car, and they sold it to him, right then. A family member picked Cynthia and her mother up and took them to a car lot. They put the $100 down on a new Maverick, their first car with automatic transmission. Her mother was able to make the payments and the car was paid off in a short time. It was a miracle. God was faithful to a single mom who had not a penny to her name, and a seventeen-year-old daughter with her who believed in miracles.

My family would occasionally visit Gospel Lighthouse Church, as my father was an evangelist and we traveled around a lot. This is where I met Cynthia. She recalls, "I always admired Raymond's timid nature and watched him from the time I was twelve (1970). The first time I saw him, he was lying in the center floor of the church praying in the Spirit and I told my mother I would marry that guy someday. I admired his passion for God because it matched mine, even though I really didn't know him."

In 1972, I faced the possibility of being drafted into the army. The Vietnam War had ended and my year was included in the alternate draft, should it be needed. My number was sixty-three that year and I was ready to serve if needed. That never happened but I fully supported those who served in defense of our great country. I love our country and military and I was privileged to be under two retired officers in ROTC during high school. Of the two officers, one was a sergeant and the other a major. It was an honor to be close to Ft. Hood and have the army officers come and do our yearly inspection. I'm grateful for that training afforded to me.

Cynthia was a sophomore in high school (four years younger than me), when she asked me to take her home from youth choir one night (1974). I took her, her cousin and best friend home also. I had two tickets to an Andrae Crouch concert for the weekend, and asked her if she would come with me. She said, "Yes, with my mother's permission". Having that permission, we had our first date. That began two years of courting and getting to know each other. We discussed our goals and morals, and they were both so similar; we had so much in common.

Cynthia graduated from high school in May 1976, and we were married June 18, 1976.

With God's help, we broke the cycle of divorce in our generation. We have a daughter and son, a son-in-law and a daughter-in-law, and nine grandchildren, six on this earth and three in heaven. We have a host of family and friends we love. We are blessed.

We have traveled the world doing missions work and actively showing love to God's people. Our goals at this time are to evangelize as many people as possible, reach our city and share the good news of Jesus where ever we go.

We love people and our country. People are God's business, so I guess you could say we are in God's business.

CHAPTER 2*

Our Children...
Miracle Births

Behold, children are a heritage from the Lord,
The fruit of the womb is a reward.
PSALM 127:3 (NKJV)

Cynthia and I have two children. We were blessed with our first child, Melissa Anne, born May 13, 1978, and our second child, Aaron Ray, born November 5, 1980. Now a family of four, we were beyond blessed and filled with thanksgiving.

Melissa Anne

(As recounted by Cynthia) I was at the end of my pregnancy with Melissa and I had been somewhat fearful of delivery. We were in a church service one night when an evangelist was praying for people. I

15

knew it was the season to release the fear that had been plaguing me. I went to the altar to be prayed for and when the evangelist laid hands on me I fell back in the arms of Jesus. It was as though I landed on a pillow. I laid there releasing the fear and anxiety to God. In a few short days I went for my doctor appointment in Dallas and he announced I was dilated to a five. He told me he thought I was in pre-labor and if I didn't go full labor that night, he wanted me at the hospital at 7:00 AM the next morning to induce labor. My sister stayed the night with us, but nothing more happened. At 7:00 AM we were at the hospital for labor to be induced. Raymond dropped me off and I walked into the labor and delivery area. The nurse came out and asked if I was in labor and I told her no, that I was just waiting for my husband. She asked if I was Mrs. Frizzelle and I told her I was. She then told me the doctor was waiting for me and they took me into a room and got everything ready. Raymond checked me in and did the last-minute paperwork. Medication to induce labor (Pitocin) was given to me, and immediately labor began. I told the nurse I felt like the baby was coming and I wanted my husband with me, but she assured me we had plenty of time, telling me, "It's your first baby, and they usually take a while." I began to insist she check me because I felt the baby coming.. sure enough the head was crowning. Raymond "flew" through the door as he finished putting on his scrubs and was seated at the back of my head. The doctor commented, "Wow, this baby didn't waste any time." My sweet husband became faint in all the excitement, so they had him step outside and put a wet cloth on his head and gave him orange juice. He came back in and we had our new baby girl, born at 8:50 AM, 7 lbs. 2oz. Yes, a miracle birth.

Aaron Ray

(As recounted by Cynthia) Melissa was almost two when we decided we wanted another child. On February 14, 1980, we joined hands and prayed and agreed that God would give us a son and we would name him Aaron Ray. We conceived. During my fourth month of pregnancy we were in the middle of moving (imagine that for those of you who know us) and I was climbing up on a counter to put away dishes. I felt something pour down my legs, and after checking, found I was bleeding heavily. I called the doctor and he told me he thought I was having a miscarriage. He ordered me to bed, and then said I should come into his office first thing the next morning and we would discuss what must be done. It was such a difficult night for us and I was so sad.

The next day Raymond took me to the doctor and I was examined. To his and our surprise, I was still pregnant. He ordered a sonogram and sure enough our baby was just fine. What he discovered was that I had placenta previa (occurs when a baby's placenta partially or totally covers the mother's cervix). Throughout the pregnancy I had so many issues with bleeding and scary moments that I thought I was going into early labor, but I never did.

During my pregnancy, I had a call from a friend I had gone to school with, letting me know she had lost her baby from placenta previa. I was grateful to know she was well, but knew we would need another miracle. Fourteen days from my due date I began to have a few more bleeding issues, so I went to see the doctor. His associate saw me that day and he wasn't aware of my issues with bleeding. Shocked, he said, "Wow, this isn't good, but you are not in labor and you are not dilated at all." He told me I probably had two more weeks to go. Very disappointed, I went to visit a friend that afternoon. She had just had her son. Then I went to vote for President Regan. (They let me go to the front of the line!) After that, I went to the grocery store and picked up some items for us. When I finally got home with little Melissa (she was two and a half then), I got ready for a hot shower and called my regular doctor to tell him I was bleeding again. He told me to get off my feet and relax, or I would go into labor soon. If the bleeding persisted, he wanted me to see me in his office.

That evening, every few minutes, Melissa kept coming in and telling me how many votes President Regan had. I knew her daddy put her up to that, trying to get my mind off my worries and the labor. We later went to bed for the night. I was awakened around 1:00 AM, continuing to hemorrhage, so I called the doctor. He told me he thought I needed to go on in to the hospital. I woke Raymond and grabbed Melissa in a blanket, and called my mom and step-dad. I asked them to meet us at the hospital, telling them I was going to be checked to see if all was well. To my surprise, my water broke. The nurse came to greet us with a wheelchair and asked how far apart my contractions were coming. I reported I was not having contractions, but that my water had broken. They took me upstairs and put me into bed. The nurse checked me and found I was at a "10". My mom stuck her head in the door to snap a picture and I told her, "Mother, I'm a 10". She quickly replied, "What? You just got here. How far apart are your contractions?" I then told her I wasn't having any contractions. This was part of our miracle. The doctor came in and reported I was ready to go. By this time my sweet husband was on the floor about to pass out. They put a cold cloth on his neck and he revived enough to go into the delivery room with me. When we got in there, the doctor told me to give a big push with the next contraction. I told him I wasn't having any contractions, so he said, "I'll give you a little help." He popped a shot of Potocin in my left leg and repeated, "Now give me a big push." Within a few pushes, we had the gift of our new baby boy. Aaron Ray entered this world at 8:52 AM, weighing 8 lbs 12 oz, no c-section needed, no emergency birth, no complications at all at the time of birth…a miracle for sure.

To God be the glory, great things He has done.

CHAPTER 3*

Bible School Miracles

I beseech you therefore, brethren, by the mercies of God,
that you present your bodies a living sacrifice, holy,
acceptable to God, which is your reasonable service..
ROMANS 12:1 (NKJV)

Financial/Miracles

In 1983 God spoke to me to step out and begin Bible School at Christ for the Nations in Dallas, Texas. After seeking God for six months, we had confirmation through a visiting minister who called us and three other couples out in a Sunday service and confirmed what God was speaking to our hearts. (This was his first visit to Gospel Lighthouse.) At the time I was working at the U.S. Post Office, where

I had been employed since 1978, which was the last year of the "no lay off clause". Most of my friends thought I was crazy for quitting. We took the step of faith and then…the storm came.

I had gotten a part time job at a company that made dental surgical tools, earning $10 an hour. That ended six weeks into the first semester of school as company sales declined. I then got a job at UPS, making $8 an hour. After my probation period, hours were cut, forcing me to make another job change. My next job, doing maintenance for a company, paid $6 an hour; all our plans were falling apart. We had rented our house for the payments we were making on it, and moved into cheaper housing on campus. My retirement funds had taken care of our first semester, but plans for our second semester were not coming together…we needed $4000.

We still attended Gospel Lighthouse and served as volunteer children's pastors. Miracle healings, salvations and growth were happening there. As the semester ended I was desperate to hear from God. We were not financially ready for our second semester. Cynthia and the kids spent three days visiting her sister in Lewisville, Texas. I spent those three days fasting to seek God for an answer. We had no money to move off campus or to stay on campus. During those three days God supernaturally spoke to me that He would take care of everything. His peace saturated my life and spirit. Cynthia did not understand that day, but three days later God spoke the same peace to her heart while she was driving. Weeping, she had to pull over and stop the car. We never looked back, but trusted God. The school allowed us to stay and we moved forward in faith.

On the first day of school of the second semester, an ex-boss called me and said God had asked him to give us $500 to pay on our school bill. In church that Sunday, he gave us that money. Someone else also gave us the funds for all our books; we were on our way. Each miracle offering came in until we only lacked $1000 of the $4000 that was due for school and housing. We attended a Christ for the Nations' Tuesday night school service. An offering was being taken for the New York campus school. With only $34 in the bank and a wife and two children to take care of, God spoke to me to give $20 of that $34, leaving us $14. At first, I hesitated, and Cynthia asked me what was wrong. I told her, "I think we are supposed to give $20." She agreed, so she wrote the check and I put it in an envelope, marking on the back, "Seed for a thousand dollars." Cynthia asked me why I wrote that on the envelope. A week and a half later, our final payment was due, and we needed that money. The Lord dropped in my heart that we would receive some more on our bill.

On Sundays, we were always in children's church, so we went to Sunday night services. That particular night the service was wonderful and we prayed together for quite some time. As we were leaving our church prayer room, the enemy spoke to me and said, "You will receive nothing tonight." I spoke out, "Satan, I don't care, God will meet our needs." As we came out of the prayer room, a couple was waiting on us and handed us $200 to be applied to our schooling expense. By the next Friday deadline, an anonymous $40 came in, and with several other gifts we had received, we had the final $1000 to pay on our school loan. God is faithful. This was only the beginning of "stepping out on water..."

And my God shall supply all your need according to His riches in glory by Christ Jesus.
PHILIPPIANS 4:19 (NKJV)

Food Provision/Miracles

During our stay at Christ for the Nations there were many financial obstacles. I was a full-time student, we had two very young children, and Cynthia tried to attend classes as much as possible.

After being there for only a short time, we were asked to be Family Assistants, meaning we would primarily oversee our apartment complex and plan events, etc. The first one we were in charge of was the entire apartment complex Christmas Party. Cynthia coordinated it and signed people up for various foods to bring. She was usually overzealous about a party so volunteered to bring cheese dip for the whole complex. How in the world would that happen with our very very limited finances? She tells the story best.

(As recounted by Cynthia) "What was I thinking? As I returned to our tiny apartment I put the kids down for a nap and sunk into the couch with sadness. I said, "Oh Father, how am I going to afford cheese dip for such a large crowd?" I actually was having a pity party and crying to God when my neighbor knocked at the door. Drying my eyes as to not let her see me having a breakdown over cheese, I answered the door. She said, "Cynthia, get your coat on and come out here, there's a truck down there loaded with stuff being given away." I wasn't at all interested and I had just put the kids down for a nap. I said, "No, I'm really not interested." She said, "Come On!" I locked the door, turned to the right and walked down a few steps, looking at a huge truck with a man inside it. As we approached the truck, he turned, with boxes in his arms and said, "Ladies, could you use some cheese?" I stood there in shock. "What?" He asked, "Would 5 lbs. each be enough?" It was state commodities that were being handed out. I've never seen a truck like it in my lifetime nor have I ever been given a box of cheese like that since.

24

It was a miracle of provision. The other interesting part of the miracle is that my neighbor was a vegetarian. Neither she nor her family ate dairy products, so she gave me her 5 lbs. of cheese. God provided the cheese I needed.

Another day, same apartment, I was in my little kitchen trying to figure out an inexpensive meal for our family and I looked at my tiered copper baskets (some of you may remember having one) used to display apples, oranges and bananas. But guess what? My baskets were empty. I was crying again, another pity party, I guess, and I said, "Oh Lord, I don't even have apples, oranges or bananas in my baskets." Then there was a knock at the door, and as was my habit there at the apartment, I looked out the window to see who was there. Not seeing anyone, I gradually opened the door, but no one was there, but guess what was there? I found a brown paper sack with apples, oranges and bananas on top! I brought it in and carefully took everything out, finding that not only did it have the delicious fruits in it I was talking to the Lord about, *but* there were also canned meats and dried items for several meals. Yes, another miracle.

But Jesus said, "Let the little children come to Me, and do not forbid them; for of such is the kingdom of heaven."
MATTHEW 19:14 (NKJV)

Among the Children/Miracles

Cynthia and I served in children's ministries for many years. She taught children's classes while we were in Bible School, and we served as Children's Pastors for multiple years. We know from experience, over and over, the absolute truth of the scripture:

Truly I tell you, unless you change and become like little children, you will never enter the kingdom of heaven. Therefore, whoever takes the lowly position of this child is the greatest in the kingdom of heaven.
MATTHEW 18: 2-4 NKJV

We have had some precious times working in ministry with children and we have seen "Miracles Among Children".

While we were at Christ for the Nations, Cynthia was asked to teach a pre-school class. The school's director thought Cynthia was a natural at teaching and assigned her a class of thirty-three, three year olds, with two assistants to help. She greatly enjoyed sharing the Bible with children, and her most enjoyable session of a day was praise and worship with the Bible lesson. Two particular sessions with these children continue to be close to our hearts.

(As Cynthia recounts) This particular day the lesson was on Peter and Cornelius (Acts 10). As I studied and prepared, the Holy Spirit began to instruct me to step aside and not limit that day's session to the ordinary of the day. Each morning was somewhat different, but very predictable in order to provide consistency for the children. When you have thirty-three three year olds in a classroom, it can be unsettling. Pre-session activities (lace up cards, puzzles, play dough or library books) were always ready for the children as they arrived. Upon arriving that day, the children seemed anxious as well as excited about the day. Around 8:15 AM we began putting away the morning pre-session items and gathered into our praise and worship circle. Every child had a blonde wooden chair in the circle and in the center there was a huge oval rug we sometimes called our prayer rug. Each child enjoyed praise and worship in his/her own special way that was natural to that particular child. All of them enjoyed it and we sang for about fifteen to twenty minutes (longer than most people would think). We took prayer requests and at that moment a huge water bug ran across the wall. The children began to scream and rustled around. I knew and recognized immediately the enemy was causing a huge distraction.

Knowing the Holy Spirit was moments from showing up, I instructed my two assistant teachers to take the bug away, help me regain structure, calm the children, and pray over the classroom. This was a big time in the lives of these children.

We completed prayer requests and went quickly to the Bible Story. As I began to tell about Peter visiting the house of Cornelius and how they were Gentiles and didn't believe in the Holy Spirit, the Holy Spirit began to move. I shared with the children how Peter thought to himself that the Gentiles were not able to receive the Holy Spirit and then God gave him a dream and told him not to call unclean what He had called clean. At that very moment, I directed my assistants to begin to intercede for every child and pray that all would begin to speak in other tongues as the Spirit spoke through them. I cautioned them that we were not to hesitate to believe and not limit what the Holy Spirit was speaking. I wrapped up the story and told the children that the Holy Spirit had a special gift to give each of them and encouraged them to speak what He gave them. I had my assistants lay hands on their heads and repeat to each child, "Receive the Holy Spirit!" As hands were laid on their heads, each three-year-old child began to speak in another language. The Holy Spirit was so powerful in speaking a new language through every little child. There was one little boy that went down and lay flat on his back on the prayer rug. He was a child that had encountered a lot of sad things in his short three years and never talked much or interacted with the other children. But this time, each child came over and laid hands on him and prayed in another language over him. It was so evident that the Holy Spirit had special instruction for this child, he being the only one that did not open his mouth. It was only a short time, but it certainly was a Holy Spirit moment time. I had witnessed a miracle.

The next year the school's director assigned me to teach kindergarten with a co-teacher. Our large room was next to the adult Bible Class. Often, we could hear them and they could hear us. As the students arrived in the mornings, they would go to their pre-session area of the classroom. On this particular morning, our student who came from China, came running into the classroom. She was usually pretty solemn, but today was crying. Her mom relayed to us that she had a heavy heart for her grandparents who were Buddhists in China. My co-teacher began to pray with her and then suddenly the entire class joined her in praying. Many of the children were crying and sobbing. My co-teacher told the children we were praying for their classmate's grandparents in China to come to know Jesus and as the crying began to be very heavy she spoke to the boys and girls telling them, "We have asked the Holy Spirit to send warring angels to China for these grandparents. Now we must thank the Holy Spirit for the great work done. Praise Him, thank Him." The crying suddenly turned to shouting praises, dancing, laughing and laughing. We all knew the work was done. After class that day, the parents that had been in the Bible Class next door to us asked, "What was going on in here today?" We shared that our class had been deep in intercession and suddenly it had turned to laughing, praising and shouting. The children chimed in to tell the good news that the grandparents in China would be saved. Many weeks passed in the school year and one morning our precious little student came bouncing into the classroom proclaiming, "Hey everyone, my grandparents in China called my mom and told her they know Jesus now!" Yes, a miracle.

During our time as children's pastors at Gospel Lighthouse in Dallas, we had church camps for children. At this one particular camp, we had well over one hundred children and a special visitation of the Holy Spirit. No one person could have planned or anticipated what happened. The Holy Spirit fell mightily among the children in the altar seeking God. Well over one hundred children received the baptism in the Holy Spirit with evidence of speaking in other tongues as the Spirit gave utterance...some at the altar and others in their dorm rooms. Two boys had visions, one of Jesus with three rings of Angels surrounding him and the other of the rapture of the church. We are so grateful for Acts 2:17-18 that confirms the Holy Spirit is for us and our children...

And it shall come to pass in the last days, says God, That I will pour out of My Spirit on all flesh; Your sons and your daughters shall prophesy, your young men shall see visions, Your old men shall dream dreams. And on My menservants and on My maidservants I will pour out My Spirit in those days; And they shall prophesy.

The summer after Bible School, we had the privilege of ministering in a spirit filled Methodist Church and that weekend many children were filled with the Holy Spirit as we taught and prayed with them. If we believe, all things are possible. Seek Him and He will fill you. I urge you to believe and have faith to teach the children in your life. Do not under estimate how God would use you to impact their little lives for the kingdom.

CHAPTER 4*

Missions Ministry Miracles

Then He said to His disciples, "The harvest truly is plentiful, but the laborers are few. Therefore pray the Lord of the harvest to send out laborers into His harvest."
MATTHEW 9:37-38 (NKJV)

In 1980, still attending Gospel Lighthouse in Dallas, Texas, and serving as volunteer Children's Pastors (since 1977), we began to step out in missions work that would take us through twenty plus years of work activity in missions and would include missions trips within the United States as well as to other countries (The Bahamas, China, Chuuk Islands, Haiti, Honduras, Mexico, Russia). We have been privileged to love God's people all over the world.

Miracles in Ministry to Micronesians

Go therefore and make disciples of all the nations,
baptizing them in the name of the Father and of the Son
and of the Holy Spirit, ...

MATTHEW 28:19 (NKJV)

We first worked with an organization called Beyond the Reef that ministered to Micronesian people from the South Pacific Islands who populated an area in Aurora, Oregon. Numerous times over the summers (beginning in 1980) we would serve with Beyond the Reef for one or two-week periods, training the children and doing work projects. One of the miracles we experienced each summer involved teaching through a group of interpreters (in several Island languages) at the same time. We taught songs in English for a week or two, and in the main service we had at the end of that time, the children would sing in perfect English, but still could not speak English.

Miracle Move to Oregon

In 1984, we were asked to join the staff of Beyond the Reef. In a leap of faith, we planned the move to Aurora, Oregon. We had no experience itinerating and raising money. Our home church pledged to give us $500 monthly support and the rest of our provision would come in monthly miracles. As we prepared to move from Dallas, we rented our home out and paid all our bills. We saved a few hundred dollars and put a deposit on our rental truck. The church committed to take an offering to assist us in our move but we had no idea what would come in, but asked God for $3000 to move our family of four a distance of twenty-six hundred miles from Dallas. I had shared a little about the move we were making, and then turned it over to God, with only heaven knowing our needs. (I actually paid our tithe that morning and put all we had left in the offering.) That night, we were given a check for $3,000. Only God, through His people, could provide this miracle. We went the next day and paid the rest on our truck. After packing, we received a call that the church had received more money that day for us ($1700) and we were asked to pick it up as we started out for Oregon. Again, God showing us He is always more than enough. We stepped out on the waters of the unknown, heading to Oregon, excited about taking this step of faith beyond our world.

During our first three months in Aurora, we lived in a two-room cabin with no running water and only a small electric heater. We took showers in a shower house and ate all of our meals in the kitchen that served all the islanders and the ministry families. The last three months we lived in the basement of a friend's house. All the funds we needed to live over this time came in just as they were needed.

The Miracle Bus Trip

A short time after our move to Oregon, Cynthia's mother relayed the news she would be having surgery (a hysterectomy) and was suffering with many health issues related to that. Cynthia began to make plans for her and our children to travel by bus back to Dallas to be with her mother for the scheduled surgery. Tickets were very reasonable and the children rode free. The only condition we were not informed of was that both children would have to sit and sleep on Cynthia's lap while traveling, unless there were extra seats on the bus.

(Recounted by Cynthia) I felt prepared for the trip. I had pillows, blankets, a suitcase, a cooler of food and all other things we needed for the journey. I had never been on a long trip on a Greyhound Bus. There was a bit of excitement, but also anxious anticipation of what lay ahead.

Little did I know the miracles I would encounter on this long journey. I became prayer partners with an African American lady traveling on the bus. We saw God move among this bus full of people on this journey …even some miracles.

There were many needy people on the bus with no provisions for food or drink. Remember, I brought a cooler with food and I fed a large portion of the people on the bus bologna and peanut butter sandwiches. I put them together and my new friend handed them out. It was like loaves and fishes…there was more than enough and some left over. (Miracle noted.)

I was told the trip was a straight shot two-and-a-half-day trip with few stops (not so!) We had to stop and "dismount" nine times the first day, one issue after another. We got stuck in the mountains (just had to sit there) for several hours while there was blasting with dynamite. The bus had several breakdowns or over heating in the high desert area. One of the nights while we were stopped, Aaron said he was sick. I felt that he was travel sick. We unloaded from the bus in the middle of the night, and Aaron started throwing up. I prayed, "Oh Father, I need your help. I can't travel with a sick child." Our nighttime layover was long enough for me to clean him up, put a cool cloth on him and see him soon feel well again. Thank you, Jesus…we continued on the trip.

The next morning a young mother with a new born baby boarded the bus. She was running from someone or some situation. My prayer partner and I tried to talk to her, but she would not talk. We both just sat in our seats and prayed. At sunrise, we stopped at a restaurant. Most people had no money to buy food, so they gave them free coffee. My prayer partner and I watched the young mother with her baby, and saw she had no money either. We ordered her a plate of food and a glass of milk to be given to her at the table where she sat. She ate all the food and put the milk in the baby's bottle. Another of God's provisions. We arrived in Dallas. My feet were swollen and looked like elephant feet from the kids sitting and sleeping on me for two and a half days; I was so glad we had arrived and the bus trip to get there was over.

The stay in Dallas was full of hard days. Mother experienced complications with the surgery and I found I had no money left to travel back home to Oregon. (I also decided to lighten my load home and leave the cooler and not take food.) I took a pillow and a blanket with us, and the suitcase was put underneath the bus with other passenger luggage. PaPa took us to the bus stop in downtown Dallas. The children and I boarded the bus with no food, no cooler and not a dime on us. I had contacted Raymond and he was to wire money to me in Colorado at the next day's stop. Upon arriving in Colorado, there was no wire, so no money. I didn't have money to call him, so I borrowed a phone and told him the money had not arrived. He was so very concerned, but I knew God would provide.

The children and I boarded the bus once again, and a gentleman in a suit got on and sat in the seat beside me. (It was unusual to see anyone dressed up to travel on a bus.) I made it a point of introducing myself to every driver and letting each one know I was traveling by myself with two small children and to look out for us. As I was reflecting over the trip back to the bus station I realized I should have borrowed money from PaPa, as I was stuck with the long journey back... no provisions for my children or myself. The man in the suit, sitting beside me, turned to me and said, "I'm supposed to give you this". He handed me $50. I didn't know what to say. He couldn't possibly have known the need. No one but God and Raymond knew that I had nothing in my billfold. The bus had an emergency stop for one of many reasons, and I guess he got off. I never saw him again or knew who he was, except my own personal angel. (Miracle noted.) When we arrived at the next food stop (restaurant) I ordered food for us. We ate plenty and took some snacks and bottled drinks with us. God is so good and He always watches over His children.

The next night a lady got on the bus with only one thing in her hand, a photo album. I sat next to her with my two sleeping children on my lap and she cried and cried into the night. I was so very tired and needed rest for the remaining journey, but somehow God gave me the strength to ask her what was wrong. She told me she had just buried her baby boy who had died unexpectedly of SIDS. She was running as far away from life as she could. Her own religion had told her he wasn't saved and he was doomed for hell. She had NO hope. That night, on a crowded bus in Salt Lake City, Utah, I was able to tell her she would see that baby again. God used an exhausted momma, holding her own two babies on an overcrowded bus in the middle of the mountains, to give hope to the hopeless. I prayed over her and told her of the love of Jesus. You never know when God is going to use you, with swollen feet and angel money in your pocket, to tell someone of His love.

Melissa's Visions

We worked among these Micronesian people and their families, teaching and training them in God's Word. During this time, our five-year-old daughter, Melissa, had two special visions. The first one was about going to China (she had never seen or heard of China) and told Cynthia and me that she was going there for missions work someday. She described the dream and the people she saw in it…it all fit China, perfectly. The other one was about Heaven. She saw the streets of gold described in Revelation. She said the streets were like clear gold. She also saw several of our friends in Heaven.

Back to Texas

Our hearts rejoiced at the miracles God was doing and showing our family. However, at the end of six months, God woke me up three mornings in a row at 4:30 AM, confirming that our work there was complete and gave me release to return home, as He had work for us to do there. So, at the end of the six months, we returned to Dallas and our church, Gospel Lighthouse.

Once home, we settled in and made ourselves available for what God would show us He wanted us to do. Leading others to Christ and ministering to the down-and-out was always on our hearts. We soon found a ministry need among some North Vietnamese refugee children. We were put in contact with a man and his wife (she was from Cambodia) who had taken many of these refugees into their home and were giving them a safe place to live, be fed and nurtured here in America. He asked if we would be available to come every Saturday to their house and minister Jesus Christ to the children. We were thrilled with this opportunity to minister to children. We also ministered on Friday nights to homeless people and prostitutes in downtown Dallas whose shelter was under bridges and in burned out buildings. We also came to know many of the adult refugees who had run for their lives in coming to America.

Anything we were part of in ministry, we had our children with us if possible. On Saturdays, wherever we ministered, Melissa and Aaron would lead songs and repeat scripture verses with the children; we were in ministry as a family.

In 1986, we began to serve as part time Children's Pastors at Memorial Assembly of God Church in Duncanville, Texas. We were paid a small stipend to work in children's ministry. This was a new ministry in their church so there was lots of excitement as we started this new venture.

We gathered with the children in the fireside room during church services. God moved in a mighty way from the beginning of our ministry with the children. There was one boy in particular who had lots of problems. His brother was known as a juvenile delinquent and had problems also, but he did not come to our services.

I was deep in prayer about how to deal with this child when the Holy Spirit instructed me to give the boy a job for children's church and to reward him for the work he did. The plan was for him to arrive early, set up the chairs in correct order and then to stay after service and take everything down. That became his job; he was a different child from that time on.

After we left that ministry, that boy, now a young man, wrote us the sweetest letter thanking us for believing in him and telling us what a difference we had made in his life. Knowing what God had done for him, we thankfully gave all glory to Him.

There were many saved, filled with the Holy Spirit, healed and called into ministry. Some who are in ministry today contact us through Facebook and let us know what God has done in and through their lives and ministry. Again, we give all the glory to God, who has done great things.

Miracle of Transportation to Oregon

In 1988, we moved to Duncan, Oklahoma to serve at Gospel Beams Church as Associate/Youth/Children's Pastors. In addition, we continued to serve with the Beyond the Reef organization for several weeks in the summers. In 1989, we began praying together for God to provide for our family of four to make the trip that summer to again serve.

By May, nothing had happened and we couldn't afford a bus or train ticket to get us all there. We just kept believing and asking. God, by the end of May, had provided two plane tickets. The story of how He did it is a fascinating recount of a miracle.

The Wednesday before our scheduled Friday departure, my wife felt the Lord speak to her and tell her to, "Get ready!". We had decided Melissa and I would go and Cynthia and Aaron would come as God worked things out. She got our clothes ready, and on Friday when Melissa and I left, I said to her, by faith, "See you in Oregon", and drove to the airport. We had a stop in Denver before flying on to Portland. In Denver, while we were waiting to board, an announcement was made that four passengers were needed to change planes, and to please come to the desk if interested. I went to the desk and offered our two tickets. My offer was accepted and in return, I was given two free round trip tickets which would be waiting in Salt Lake City when the plane arrived. With Melissa in hand, we hurried to catch another plane, and flew to Salt Lake City. Upon arriving, I received the tickets and asked when I could use them. They said, "Immediately!" My heart leaped for joy at God's answer and provision. I could hardly wait to tell my wife. We arrived in Portland, Oregon, only fifty-five minutes later than our original flight. I was not able to reach Cynthia, so I went ahead and booked the flight for her and Aaron and put them in overnight mail. When I reached her, at a friend's house, and asked if she was ready, her heart rejoiced as I told her the story. In less than 24 hours, she was in Oregon and we served that two weeks together with our children and experienced God's miracle power. When it was time, we all flew home together.

The Garden Miracle

In 1990, we were still living in Duncan, Oklahoma and continued to be involved in missions ministry as well as on staff at Gospel Beams Church, still believing for God's provisions for our family of four. We lived in a small house on the church property. The church also owned the property across the parking lot from our house, and we had been given permission to use it. Cynthia was homeschooling both of our children, Melissa (twelve yrs. old) and Aaron (almost ten yrs. old), and we decided to plant a garden and teach them how to care for it. The neighbors across the street came quickly to let us know it would NEVER work to have a garden there because a house used to be there and there were rocks, bricks and unlevel ground to plant in and NOTHING would thrive. We were also told if we did plant a garden and didn't fence it in, people would steal us blind.

We decided to plant it anyway. We walked around the garden, prayed over it and asked God to give us an abundant harvest. Days turned into weeks and we began to have the most amazing garden anyone had ever seen. The okra plants grew to be twelve feet tall and Cynthia and the kids would have to get the ladder to pick the top sections. Squash and tomatoes produced and produced along with the rest of things planted in our garden (cantaloupe, cucumbers, water melons, onions and carrots).

The neighbors once again came over to view the abundance and asked what we were putting on our squash to keep the bugs off and we told him, "Just rabbit poop!" (We were also raising rabbits in our small back yard.) He asked if we would go look at his squash plants. We walked over with him to see dried up, bug-eaten plants. He asked us what we thought he could do. We told him we had just prayed over our garden and God took care of it.

The rest of the story is that we had tomatoes way into October. We shared a lot of the tomatoes with our neighbor's wife who made salsa. We kept taking her tomatoes by the bags and she and her husband just looked in amazement at what God was doing. One year we had tomatoes into November and I finally cut them down, giving the green ones away. God always blesses what we give to Him. Neighbors and church people watered and took care of our gardens when we made our summer mission trips to Oregon.

Chuuk Trip Miracle

The summer of 1990 we were given the opportunity to go the Chuuk Islands (formerly Truk Islands or Hogoleu Islands, cluster of sixteen much eroded high volcanic islands in the Federated States of Micronesia, western Pacific Ocean). The nineteen-day trip would include stopping at three other Micronesian Islands, but our stay was to be on Chuuk. Having ministered to the Micronesian people in Aurora, Oregon, during previous summers, and having lived there for six months, we were familiar with their culture, language and food. We just needed the two tickets to get there and then to return home. Someone in our church purchased both our tickets (miracle noted). We arranged for our two children to stay with family. God made provisions for all the details in our absence, and provided for the strength and peace for Cynthia, who had a few issues with flying that long distance, to make the trip (miracles noted).

Upon arriving on the Island of Chuuk, we were given a written handout stating there was an outbreak of cholera on the Island, and a list of things to avoid (including shell fish and eggs). We began to pray as a team for God's supernatural protection over all of us. Not one of

41

us contacted any illnesses throughout our stay on the Island (and our first meal was egg sandwiches)!

The many, many children we were to minister to was unreal. The whole Island seemed to have received the news we were there. The small wooden framed shanties where we held services hardly had room enough for all of us as the Gospel was shared, altar calls were given, and we prayed for the sick. But God's ways are not our ways; there were many, many children who asked Jesus into their hearts and many were healed and delivered in the days we were there (miracles noted).

There were some people on the island who could not make it to the other side of the Island to the main churches and classes where we were. We were asked to go into those villages and hold services for those people. Cynthia and I had taken very little money for the trip, depending on our meals and provisions from the team's offerings. We went to the small village designated for us, where we sang, preached and prayed for the sick. This very, very poor community took up an offering for us in the amount of $134. We did not want to take the offering gift, but their customs did not allow refusal. We were both completely blown away with gratefulness as to how God used two passionate people to teach the Gospel and then allowed us to receive a gift from the most unlikely of people. That's the way God does things. He asks for what is in your hand, then takes it and multiplies it according to His will. Never underestimate God's ways. They are beyond human understanding. We continued working with Micronesian people in the summers through the Beyond the Reef organization until we accepted a call to another church in 1992.

Children's Ministry to the Streets:
A Dream Come True

"For the word of the Lord is right,
And all His work is done in truth.
He loves righteousness and justice;
The earth is full of the goodness of the Lord"

PSALM 33:4-5 (NKJV)

In 1992 we moved to Lawton, Oklahoma, to become Children's Pastors and Christian Education Directors at Lawton First Assembly of God. We were not full-time staff that first year, but God was faithful in His provision for us. I was provided a job for that year through some special friends. God gave us many dreams that unfolded during our ten years there. One of our dreams was to take children's ministry to the streets... through this church that dream came to pass.

With our pastor supporting us, we began the ministry using a temporary trailer. For the summer of 1994, we had great success with salvations and reaching families. At General Council in 1995, we discovered (S.T.I.T.C.H.E.S.) Street Ministry. Upon our return home, we presented the vision and needs to our senior pastor and the church board. It was given full support of the church with finances and volunteer workers. In September, we launched this ministry and witnessed a miracle provision for the trailer for the ministry. One Sunday morning $17,000 was given for purchase of the S.T.I.T.C.H.E.S. trailer we got from a ministry in California. It was a great blessing and included a portable sound system. With the gift of our anointed street directors and many volunteers, we started ministry at two sites and saw souls saved.

43

Over the next five years, we saw great miracles, with four thousand souls saved during that time. We did holiday gifts and a special kids camp for the children for three years with only a two-week break in August and at Christmas. No matter what the weather condition, we went out weekly. Lawton's city officials and law enforcement agency were well aware of what our street ministry was all about. We were shown documentation of a thirty-eight percent drop in crime in areas where we ministered every Saturday. God moved mightily in the "church without walls" as we ministered the love of Jesus Christ.

More Missions Ministry

While in Lawton, we worked with our church for ten years in hosting the "Heaven's Gates/Hell's Flames" drama. The church saw over ten thousand souls saved during that time. We also had opportunity to go on many mission trips. In Mexico, we built a church and had nightly services with salvations and much more through the work of the Holy Spirit. In Haiti, we saw miracles and ministered to many students at their public schools and orphanages with many salvations. Our visit to Russia was so awesome, with over three hundred in one service receiving Jesus as their personal Savior. Combined with Bethel Assembly, we had the privilege of rebuilding a church in Honduras. Our visit to the Bahamas with our son's senior class was awesome, with over five hundred salvations in the schools. We also made our first trip to China during our time at Lawton First Assembly. And that trip to China is another story of a fantastic miracle of God.

Melissa's Call to China

Therefore, my beloved brethren, be steadfast, immovable, always abounding in the work of the Lord, knowing that your labor is not in vain in the Lord.

1 CORINTHIANS 15:58 (NKJV)

Melissa's call to go to China for mission ministry did not fade through her years of growing up from the five-year-old little girl who had a dream about going to China someday. She read books about China, watched movies about it and read about missionaries that had gone there.

She shared her "calling" with family and friends and in her junior year in college (1999-2000), one of her professors who had known her all of her life helped her plan a trip to China over her spring break. The college she attended had a spring break event where students went on trips around the United States and the world. She went on the trip to China, along with several college friends, professors and people from our home church as well as the church she attended while in college. Cynthia also made the trip with her.

The group got an incredible deal through a travel company. They got a tour of Beijing, along with meeting up with the ELIC team (English Language Institute of China that had been recruiting at her university for several years.) In Beijing, they toured The Great Wall and Tiananmen Square, as well as several other famous places in China. They also went to see the Chinese acrobats and enjoyed Chinese food as well as doing one of their favorite things…shopping. On their last evening there, they went to the ELIC headquarters and met with leaders and students. They had a great time asking questions and getting a feel for what those people did. Both Cynthia and Melissa knew immediately, that was where she would go. They both felt a peace, and after all the years of praying and knowing she would go there, it was becoming a reality for Melissa.

Melissa returned home for the summer and that fall, started her senior year in college (2000-2001). She did her student teaching the second semester and was beginning to pray about what job she would take. Not even thinking about China, she went to a job fair and found interest in seven different teaching job opportunities. (Most of the jobs were in Texas and paid very well, even offering "sign on" bonuses.) As a young woman who had not yet ever had even one paying job, this was exciting for her. On yet another day when she was home sick (during the time she was doing her student teaching) she got a call from ELIC. She was asked if she was going to China. God had not forgotten His plan. She knew immediately that was what she was supposed to do. She had twenty-four hours to get her application turned in and within forty eight hours she had an over the phone interview and then started working on letters to raise money for her trip. It happened to be a year that they had scholarships ($10,000) for teachers and she had to raise only $7,000. After graduation (2001), she began sending out letters and spoke at several churches. The money, "plus some", came in immediately! It was a complete miracle. Along with all of the finances, our precious church gave her a toiletries shower, supplying her with everything she needed to last a whole year, "plus some". She knew she was right in the middle of God's will, but when the day came to depart, it was hard for her to leave her family.

The ELIC group she was with went to California for two weeks of training before going overseas to China. During her stay in California, her brother, Aaron, got engaged to his future wife, Regan. It was hard for her to miss this event and not be with her family, but she knew she was where she was supposed to be; something she knew since she was five years old.

Melissa describes her first few weeks in China as being a bit "crazy", and she seriously wanted to come home. One of the junior high students she had mentored in her youth group had died in a car accident; the first twelve days the group had no running water; then 9/11 happened. They really didn't know if they would get to stay or not. In all that craziness, there was a miracle coming. Because no one wanted to fly after 9/11, fares were cheap and both Cynthia and I and Aaron and Regan got to go to China for Christmas 2001.

Melissa was unable to meet us, so, with a huge language barrier, I had to navigate our trip to the ELIC Center. As we exited the airport, I began to try to obtain a taxi ride to take us to the Center. As we arrived at the Center, I was a little disoriented and left my briefcase in our taxi. The taxi driver realized I had left it and remembered where he had dropped us off. Inside my briefcase was $200 cash that I felt God wanted us to give to the pastor we would meet who had spent twenty years in prison for sharing the gospel. Our passports and other vital information were also in that briefcase. God put the right taxi driver in our path among thousands of people, directing the taxi driver back to us. He brought the briefcase back to me at the Center, at no charge, and refused a tip. (Miracle noted.) I knew God had protected us and the gift that we brought to the pastor. Later we had the privilege of giving the pastor the gift.

Melissa showed us around Beijing and we all took a train ride together, getting to see where she lived, her school and the city. We attended Christmas service at the Chinese church and Melissa sang a solo in Chinese. What an honor that was for her. It was very hard for us to leave, and even harder for her to see us go, but what a treasure in the middle of her year in China.

A few weeks after we left, they celebrated the Chinese holiday, and her group was able to travel. They went to Thailand for a week to meet up with others, then on to Hong Kong on a train. They went several places along the way to Xian to see the Terracotta Warriors. It was an incredible experience for all of them. When they returned to the school from traveling, only six months remained until Melissa would return home.

Melissa was in China with a team of five other people (three women and two men). They lived in apartments on campus where the Chinese teachers lived. Students also lived on the school's campus. The team taught different grades with Co-Chinese teachers. They taught their classes songs, phrases and practical English activities, like greetings, shopping, holidays, colors and numbers. (Melissa had three third grade classes, four fourth grade classes and one fifth grade class.) They built great relationships with their students and the Co- Chinese teachers. During the time the team lived there, twelve of the Chinese there came to know Jesus, one for every month she lived there. Since then they have heard of many more that accepted Christ. That made every difficult day worth it. There were many days Melissa was very homesick, but she tried to make the most of every single moment. She walked and prayed every morning and during nap time. She read through the Bible and wrote a journal entry for every single day she was there. There were no distractions like we have so many of in the United States, so it was easy to find time to do those things, as well as read a lot of books. There were also many days of fun and some of sickness; with God's grace, the team made it through them all.

(As recounted by Melissa) I'm so grateful for the opportunity I had to live in China for that year. It was one of the best, but hardest things I have ever done. Growing up with that dream in my heart, I never knew if I would be there for a year or a lifetime, but after the year I spent there, I felt complete peace that I had fulfilled what God had called me to do. Someday I would like to take my husband and children there to see where I lived and worked. What a great God we have to call a five-year-old little girl to China, keep it in her heart until she graduated from college, celebrated her twenty-third birthday and then make her trip to China.

Then He said to His disciples, "The harvest truly is plentiful, but the laborers are few. Therefore pray the Lord of the harvest to send out laborers into His harvest."
MATTHEW 9:37-38 (NKJV)

Every mission trip we took during those years had miracle provisions that covered our travel costs. Miracles manifested on every mission trip. Cynthia and I are still "Missions Minded" and look forward to the opportunities to have missionaries as guest speakers in our church, every mission trip our church youth take, and the annual Light for the Lost Banquets. We celebrate the freedom to support and encourage those called into full time missions work each year through the Missions Conventions in our church…truly, we love, support and pray for those laborers called into missions ministry.

CHAPTER 5*
Doug and Melissa's Miracles

Jesus looked at them and said, "With man this is impossible, but not with God; all things are possible with God."

MARK 10:27 (NKJV)

From the time she was a little girl, our daughter Melissa wanted to be married and be a mommy (just like her "mommy"). Little did we know the miracles it would take for her heart's desire to be realized. The enemy tried to hinder and steal that from her. We prayed for her faithfully, as well as for the man she would marry. He too would need miracles.

Medical Miracle

When she was seventeen, during the first few weeks of her senior year, we found out she had a large tumor inside of her right ovary. (We were scheduled to go on a mission's trip to Romania, but cancelled that to take care of Melissa.) Immediate medical thought was cancer and immediate medical response was to consider a hysterectomy. We took her to the doctor on a Thursday and she had major emergency surgery the next Wednesday. We rarely took her to the doctor, except for issues with hormonal related migraines that she had since she was six years old. Then, all of a sudden, she was having major surgery. She was in surgery for over four hours. An incision larger than a c-section incision was made. The doctor found that the tumor had become detached from other affected organs (evidence of what had been prayed for in our church service) and when it was removed with the right ovary, it ruptured in the doctor's hand. The tumor (the size of a cantaloupe) was a nine inch wide dermoid tumor with five cysts inside of it-- hair tissue, bone tissue, eye tissue, thyroid tissue...all kinds of interesting things. It is unknown exactly was causes these, but they start growing at birth and continue to grow until they are discovered. It was the "case" of the month in that local medical setting. The doctor told us that there was a small chance the tumor could grow back and that Melissa might not be able to have children.

She missed about a month of school in her initial post-surgery healing. Six months later, close to her graduation from high school, Cynthia took her for her six month checkup. She was just beginning to get back to "normal". As the doctor did the exam, she felt something on the right side where the tumor and ovary had been removed. Both the doctor and Cynthia were devastated, thinking the tumor had grown back. An appointment was made with a specialist for a sonogram to be done a couple of days later. Cynthia cried when they got back to the car at the thought of Melissa having to go through all of this again. Melissa comforted her mother, telling her things would be ok, that it would just be a new ovary.

God gave Melissa a special kind of grace because she never felt fear or anxiety during this entire season. They went back for the sonogram. During the procedure, the sonographer scanned everything while looking for abnormal growth on the right side. Long story short (next miracle), the sonographer showed Cynthia and Melissa the perfectly normal right ovary that had grown back. As Melissa put it, "Jesus had grown her a brand new right ovary"! It was recorded in her medical records as a miracle.

Moving On...

She did continue to deal with other health issues, including PCOS (PolyCystic Ovary Syndrome, a common hormone imbalance that affects 1 out of 10-15 women), thyroid issues, parathyroid issues, ruptured cysts, hormone imbalances and Hashimoto's disease. In spite of these health issues, Melissa moved on with her life; by God's grace, she moved forward in the steps He set before her. She graduated high school in 1996, and college in 2001. She spent a year teaching in China (2001-2002), a dream she had since early childhood. (This miracle story is recorded in Chapter 4, Missions Miracles/Melissa's Trip to China.)

Melissa moved back to Lawton when she returned from China and secured a job teaching fourth grade. She lived with us. The following February Cynthia and I moved to Miami, Oklahoma, to pastor Miami First Assembly of God. Melissa finished the school year in Lawton, then moved to Miami and lived with us for a season, serving as support in numerous ministry areas for us at Miami First. In the fall of 2003, she accepted a job teaching school in Bluejacket, Oklahoma, and supplemented her income with private music lessons and employment at a restaurant in Grove, Oklahoma. She served as interim children's pastor at Miami First over the summer (2004) and went to Kids Camp at Turner Falls Campgrounds in July. There, she met and made new friends…also met a young man named Doug Young, a youth pastor in Bristow. Dating someone else at the time and soon moving to Red Oak, Texas, where she had accepted a teaching position for the 2004-05 school year, left no time for them to "connect". Melissa best tells the story that led to the beginning and establishment of the "Young Family"…the miracle was unfolding.

The Beginning (Doug and Melissa)

(As recounted by Melissa) A mutual friend from camp that summer called and asked if she could give Doug Young my phone number. I didn't remember much about him, so thought nothing of it when I didn't hear from him. Then came November. The week before Thanksgiving, I got very sick, could not stop throwing up and ended up at the ER. I got a call from Doug Young and had to apologize and ask him to call me later because I was throwing up. I was in the hospital for almost a week and we talked on the phone, every single evening. My mom came to Texas to take me to Miami to spend Thanksgiving with our family. On our way to Oklahoma, Doug called me and asked if he could take me out on Friday, if I felt up to it. I said yes.

He arrived with flowers and we went out to eat, then back to my folks' house. We talked and visited with my parents for the rest of the evening. He asked if he could take me out again on Monday. We considered that Monday our first official date since I was feeling better. We went to Joplin, ate at Olive Garden and then to a movie (National Treasure). We continued a long-distance relationship, as I taught in

Texas and he lived/worked in Oklahoma. In May, he came to see me on my birthday. He bought me the movie, National Treasure, took me to Olive Garden for dinner and then we went back to my apartment. I found it full of roses and candles (he had coordinated this with my best friend) and he proposed. We married on July 16, 2005, a year after we had met. We moved to Edmond, Oklahoma, where I taught elementary school, he worked for Wells Fargo Finance and we volunteered as young adult pastors at our church.

In the course of our first year and a half of marriage, I struggled with hormonal related health issues. I was put on hormones because my doctor said I wasn't producing any. I felt great at first, but then became very ill. I ended up having Doug take me to the ER, as I could not stop throwing up. Once things were under control, I went home that night and threw away all of the meds I was taking and told the Lord, if we are going to have children, He would just have to do a miracle as there was no way I could go on feeling the way I felt. Nine months later, on February 11, 2007, we found out we were pregnant with our first child.

Miracle (x 3)

We were so excited! I honestly had an amazing pregnancy. I was never sick! But I did have severe swelling. I had just started back to teaching (August) when my doctor put me on bed rest. In 24 hours, I had to do interviews to get a full-time substitute teacher and finish a ton of work in my classroom. I was a bit overwhelmed! I still had five more weeks until my due date. My labor was stopped three times during the first two and a half weeks of bed rest. Then came my 37-week appointment... I'd been on bed rest for almost 3 weeks. My doctor told me to go home and get my bags and meet her at the hospital. We called everyone and told them, "Today is the day!" We could not wait to meet our sweet boy! We thought it would all happen very quickly...but twelve hours later I ended up in an emergency c-section. Malachi Douglas was born and healthy, weighing in at 7 lbs. 12 oz.; my surgery lasted almost three hours. A lot of scar tissue from my tumor surgery, twelve years earlier, had to be removed, among other things. Even though it was a huge step of faith for us, I ended up not going back to teaching. We accepted a position with our church, and became full time staff as young adult pastors. A new season was happening in our lives.

In August of 2009, we accepted the job as children's pastors at Miami First Assembly and moved our family of three, just before Malachi turned two years old. We moved into the upstairs of my parents' house and lived there for two years. On February 11, 2010, we found out we were expecting our second child. I was actually not feeling well and had stayed home with Malachi. The pregnancy test was positive. Malachi was the first to know and immediately said, "It's going to be our Chloè!" We had always told him, when we had a girl her name would be Chloè. From that moment on, he called her Chloè and I wouldn't let anyone tell him otherwise! Sure enough, our little prophet Malachi was right! My c-section was scheduled for October 4. On October 2 (OU/TX game day) my water broke and we headed for the hospital. Chloè Anne was born healthy and weighed in at 8 lbs. 3 oz. We now had our second miracle child.

We had purchased a house during my pregnancy (same house where I went to have my wedding dress altered). We gutted and remodeled it, and moved into our new home the summer of 2011. (Chloè was 9 months old and the day we moved in, she began to crawl.) We felt so blessed with our two babies (one of each) and our new home...we had our miracle family. But God had a bonus blessing for us. On Memorial Day, 2013, we found out I was pregnant with our third child. This was a huge surprise, but we were thrilled. I had another wonderful pregnancy, and was scheduled for a c-section on Monday, January 27, 2014.

On Saturday, January 25, I started having lots of contractions and wasn't feeling too great. I had not felt like eating and later that afternoon, I decided to go to our local hospital to be monitored. My contractions were two minutes apart so I needed to go on to Tulsa hospital where my doctor was. I went home and we made our phone calls to everyone. I showered and we headed to Tulsa. My mom was not able to be with me for the births of my first two children, so I hoped and prayed she would be allowed to come back this time. My doctor was out of town, so I asked the doctor on call if my mom could come back with us, and he said yes. I was so excited! They took me back to prep me for surgery and then my mom and Doug came back.

I had never felt anything during my two-previous c-sections, but this one was a bit different...I definitely felt the tugging and pulling! Our brand-new baby boy weighed in at 10 pounds 10 ounces! This 5'4" momma was in shock. He was perfect and healthy and we took him home 36 hours later, stopping by my brother and sister-in-law's house for pizza and family time. MacPhearson Ray was a bonus miracle we didn't know we needed.

A Season of Change

We moved to the Tulsa area in July 2014, where we accepted a position as campus pastors at Woodlake Assembly of God campus in Glenpool, Oklahoma. Then in the summer of 2016, a new season began in our lives. By the end of 2016, Doug was working in management for a food chain and I was CEO for our own wholesale business.

We had found a house for the five of us, thinking we were truly blessed with our family of five. We were in total shock when we found out, (our youngest was three years old) that I was pregnant, for the fourth time. (I was literally selling all the baby items and because I was tired of dealing with all the female issues I had…I was even considering a hysterectomy.) We were excited and thrilled, with no clue to the journey ahead of us that would require and birth more faith and trust in God than we had ever known or had the need to know.

Except for the heartbeat being a little on the higher end, everything was perfect. I didn't feel sick and I hadn't gained a single pound. I thought I was doing great to be thirty-nine and pregnant with another child. I was working extremely hard with our wholesale business and Doug was working long hours with his job. All five of us went to my doctor's appointment. Malachi asked the doctor what he thought the baby was and he said he wasn't 100% sure, but thought a girl. We were so excited and would get confirmation at our next appointment.

My cousin and her kids came to stay with us for a few days to hang out and help me get some packaging done. I felt great the whole time, but woke up on Wednesday morning with some bleeding. I hoped and prayed it would be nothing. We called the doctor's office, and not getting a return call, finally headed to the ER. As we arrived, the doctor's office called and we were told to go the office immediately. My doctor was out so a PA came in to see us. She did two different sonograms and there was no movement or heartbeat. We were in shock and heartbroken. Thursdays were my doctor's surgery days, so we were scheduled to be at the hospital at 5:45 the next morning. We called our families on the way home and told our children that Jesus had taken London Grace to Heaven. There were lots of tears. My parents came to help with the care of our kids while I had surgery and then took them back to Miami for several days so I could just rest and recover. In the next few days I experienced a lot of severe pain and heavy bleeding. I finally called my doctor and he told me to go to his office the next morning. (That day was originally supposed to be our gender confirmation day.) While I lay on the table waiting, there was a baby about the same size as London on the screen. I guessed it to be from the previous sonogram. The doctor and nurse came in and he began to do a sonogram. I thought my eyes were playing tricks on me, because I'd just seen that baby on the screen, but there she was. My doctor turned pale and I honestly thought he was going to pass out. He had missed her during the surgery. He said this had never happened before. I didn't even know what to feel or think, but this meant I had to endure pain for several more days and go through the surgery, yet again!

That week was awful! It was July 4th week and Doug had to work all day. Thankfully the kids just rested with me. I started feeling very sick and woke up ill the next morning, the day before my second surgery, and ended up in the ER. They finally got the migraine and vomiting under control; I was not septic, thank the Lord. The next morning, I went in for surgery. I made it through the surgery and extra care was taken to make sure they didn't miss London this time. I took a break from our business just to try to begin to heal and deal with all that had happened.

It was getting close to the holidays and to our surprise, the week before Thanksgiving, I found out I was pregnant, for the fifth time. We were excited but still apprehensive after all we had just been through. I went to the doctor and had everything confirmed and I was so excited that we could surprise our family at Christmas with the news. We were so sad London wasn't going to be with us, so we thought this was such a blessing. But I woke up bleeding on Thanksgiving morning (2016). I had lost another baby.

In the midst of all that happened during this season of change in our lives, I chose to draw close to my family and make our home a peaceful place for us and for all who enter. I'm grateful for the friends and family God sent to encourage us and pray for us. We have three miracle children, and each year we not only celebrate their birthdays, but we celebrate them as the miracles they are. While we do not understand the loss of our last two miracle babies, we do give thanks we will see them again, in heaven. And we continue life as a family of five, seeking to "know His will and live for His glory."

Pastor Appreciation Sunday at Miami First was scheduled for October 28, 2018. Doug was scheduled as the guest speaker. He spoke about the aspects of choosing wisely and shared from his heart the grief and restoration they were experiencing during that season of their lives.

(Recounted from that sermon) Doug resigned from the ministry in the summer of 2016, and began his career in management with food service. Dealing with aspects of changing careers, working a very demanding schedule and trying to keep up with his family was not easy...then came the loss of their fourth child (London Grace), and shortly thereafter, loss of their fifth child. He reached a point he had to admit he needed some help in coping and dealing with all of this, and accepted Melissa's invitation for some counseling. He emphasized he did not understand all that happened to them or all that they were going through, especially the loss of their last two babies. He gave testimony that he couldn't imagine living his life without God, and he chose to serve God, no matter what.

Doug gave strong emphasis on focus that every day is a chance to choose wisely and use godly wisdom in making decisions:

+ choose to wake up and be willing to make choice to serve God
+ choose to serve God, every day, even in times when you feel anger
+ choose to raise your kids
+ choose to go to your job and be happy/if it is not fun, make it fun
+ choose to forgive, because you have been forgiven
+ choose to love, because you have been loved
+ choose to lead, because you have been led

In choosing wisely, he gave reminder that the greatest choice one ever makes is in accepting Jesus Christ as Savior. As he is doing in his story, he encouraged allowing God to work through your story and use it as well as allowing Him to work inside you, and to use you. He shared, "Tomorrow comes every day. Make the decision to wake up and serve God and be willing to choose wisely. In the end, others are watching the way you live; choose to make decisions based on Jesus."

In December 2018, Melissa had surgery (she chose to have a hysterectomy). She did well and recovery has brought improved health. They may never understand the loss of their last two babies, or the other difficulties and trials during that season of their lives, but they do choose to continue to serve God and give testimony to His faithfulness through it all. They remain a family of five as their miracle continues to unfold.

To God be all glory for the miracle history in their family, and the miracles yet to be experienced… (miracles to be continued!).

CHAPTER 6

Aaron and Regan's "Miracles"

And we know that all things work together for good to those who love God, to those who are the called according to His purpose.

ROMANS 8:28 (NKJV)

A aron and Regan met during their college years at Southwestern Assemblies of God University (SAGU) in Waxahachie, Texas. They became engaged late summer of 2001 and traveled with Cynthia and me to China where we spent Christmas 2001 with Melissa. Aaron did two summer internships at Lawton First Assembly in Lawton, Oklahoma, before graduating from SAGU in May 2002. He and Regan married August 3, 2002 in Lawton. Their first ministry employment was in Mustang, Oklahoma, as junior high youth pastors. During the summer of 2003 they returned to Lawton First Assembly and were on staff there as junior high youth pastors.

First Child/Move to Texas/Miscarriage

On October 7, 2004, after months and months of daily sickness, Regan gave birth to our first grandchild, Jaxon Clark. He was perfectly healthy in every way. In 2005 Regan completed work for her Bachelor's degree and graduated from Cameron University in Lawton. In 2007, they relocated to McKinney, Texas, to serve as lead youth pastors. By January 2008, we were all excited knowing they were expecting their second child, and our second grandchild. February 2008 was a month of tragedy and loss, but also of a great miracle for both Aaron and Regan. They would never be the same again.

For You formed my inward parts; You covered me in my mother's womb. I will praise You, for I am fearfully and wonderfully made; Marvelous are Your works, And that my soul knows very well.

PSALM 139:13-14 (NKJV)

(As recounted by Regan) It was February 7, 2008, and we were going in for a routine doctor's visit to check the health of our precious baby and hear that sound that every parent longs for...the HEART BEAT. We walked in and sat down in the beautiful lobby, seating our son Jaxon beside us. We read whatever magazines were available and tried to occupy our son (then three years old) who had the energy of a junior high school kid with three shots of espresso. Finally, the door opened, and someone said, "Mrs. Frizzelle, we're ready for you." We walked back to the usual room and went through the usual routine as we had done on previous appointments. Our nurse came to check the heartbeat...and in that moment, everything changed. We sat and watched the nurse check for the heartbeat and all of a sudden, her facial expression changed. She checked again and then looked at us with a false sense of confidence and said, "I'm going to grab another nurse because I might not be doing this correctly." She was gracious in the way she communicated, but we were fully aware that something was not right. The next nurse came in and said, "Let's go to another sonogram room and try another method in case we are simply missing where your baby is resting in the womb." We sat back and prepared ourselves for the unexpected. As she administered the procedure, she looked calmly into our faces and said, "I'm sorry to tell you, but this is your baby, here on the screen, and there is no heartbeat." I cannot even put into words the sick feeling we both got in our stomachs at that very moment.

(As recounted by Aaron) Up to this point, we already had more challenges than we ever needed...our family had moved to a place where we knew no one, had lost thousands of dollars on a house that took eighteen months to sell (in the state we had transitioned from) and add on the fact that the church where we were on staff had lost rights to its building by selling it before the new building was built and had gone 100% mobile church, putting our youth group in a downtown square and the main church in an elementary school across town. Given all of that together, and then lose the child that had kept us holding onto hope, and it was a recipe for emotional disaster. We walked out that day with tears in our eyes and our son Jaxon asking many different questions about what all had just happened. What we were not yet aware of was that the scariest part of this loss would not come for another twenty-four hours.

We went home, had family and friends that were aware of what was going on sit with us and pray with us as we prepared for the next day's events of Regan having a D&C (removal of the child, the placenta and any excess tissue). We lay down that night, simply praying one prayer… "God, please be near us in these moments." We were reminded of a statement that meant so much to us…"When you can't see God's hand, you can choose to trust His heart." Wow, were we going to need that in the months to come.

Surgery/Miracle

We woke up early on February 8, 2008, and went to pre-op. We walked through the motions of what we had to do and tried our best to control our self-talk, which was asking a million questions of what was going on. Our doctor had done this routine surgery hundreds of times and it was scheduled to take only twenty minutes. Today, however, was going to be different, for us all. About forty-five minutes into the surgery something happened that rattled all of us. The doctor came bursting through the doors, with blood splattered on his scrubs, and said very directly, "Mr. Frizzelle, may I see you please?" As I walked through the hallway doors that same sick gut feeling came back. Here is exactly what was told to me in about two minutes…"Mr. Frizzelle, your wife is in critical condition and we are making decisions very fast. We cannot get her uterus to close and we have tried everything. It is bleeding at a rate we cannot control and here is what we know…in ten minutes, if she does not stop bleeding we will have to do a full hysterectomy…in twelve minutes major organs in her body will be in serious trouble… and in fifteen minutes, if we cannot stop the bleeding, it is possible that we could lose her. We do not have blood on hand at this surgery center so you need to meet us at the ER just a few miles from here." He then walked quickly back to do what he could, and I returned to the waiting room where I needed to process and communicate everything that had just happened and give directions as to what we needed to do next. All I could get out before tears filled my eyes was, "They cannot stop the bleeding and we all need to head to the ER." Over the next ten to twelve minutes I called our pastor and we drove as fast we could to the other ER. When we arrived, I stood outside and watched the ambulance arrive, but there was something inside of me that could not cope with losing my wife…I could not even walk over to the loading door and watch them unload her from the ambulance. They immediately went into action to save her life and I was sent to the office to sign paperwork and talk about insurance. No one ever wants to answer those questions in the moments when life and death are a real option for someone you love (Regan was twenty-eight years old). The minutes went on and soon two hours had passed…no one could do anything but pray and wait to see what Jesus was going to do. The questions I starting thinking about were life and death serious: "What would life be like as a single dad? Would I stay in youth ministry? What would it be like having to plan a funeral for my young wife? Why is this happening to me? Did I do something that God was punishing me for? Would I get through this? What was I going to tell our son?" All I knew was that it would have been easy to let my mind go a thousand different directions if I was not careful.

The two hours passed and we all held our breath as the doctor came out. We heard the best words we could have ever asked for as the doctor said, "Mr. Frizzelle, your wife is alive and she is doing great." I can't explain the deep breath I took at that moment and how hope seemed to come back, even with a force.

My mother-in-law and I were given permission to go in and see Regan, and it was like the walk of life heading to her room. Yes, we had lost a child, but we were given another chance. We walked in and Regan began having flashbacks of what had just taken place due to the medication she was given. We all cried, laughed, took deep breaths and thanked God for the miracle of life. The attending nurses came back every thirty minutes, and one by one, stated how they had never seen someone look so close to death and yet turn around so quickly. We know the reason and He is the King of Kings and Lord of Lords and He even has the keys to death. Jesus performed a miracle that day. We were aware of the loss of our child, but because we know how much Jesus loves children, we were confident that our child would be raised by the greatest Father ever. We remain confident in that...our child is being raised by the greatest Father, EVER.

Another Miracle

We went home the next day and the first night home Regan was awakened by the Lord and told to read Hosea 1:6, and she did: **Gomer conceived again and bore a daughter.** In that moment, she felt strongly that God gave us a promise of another child. Honestly, with all the trauma we had walked through we were not in a place where we had really even started praying for another child. We just wanted to get back to a place where life felt normal again and process all the ups and downs that we had gone through. She woke me up the next morning and told me what had happened and what scripture she read. This was a promise given to us that would be what we held onto for the next year and a half.

We were instructed that over the next six months Regan would need to have blood work done monthly to make sure that what was called a molar pregnancy, which was the cause of losing our child, was not growing again. This was something that could not only cause us to lose another child, but could potentially develop into cancer. While the six months seemed like eternity, it was six months of celebrating the life of my wife.

Following that series of tests, Regan was cleared to try and get pregnant again. Within weeks of the last test she got pregnant … we were having a baby girl. The joy was overwhelming but to the equal part of that season was the fear that was overwhelming because we were going to the same hospital, seeing the same doctor and walking into the same rooms that just months ago we had walked through and experienced a very unexpected loss. I hope that even admitting that we were walking in fear is encouraging to whoever might be reading this, because it is important to be reminded that faith does not rewrite reality, it gives us hope in the middle of what is true reality.

One of the greatest challenges Regan had faced in each of her pregnancies was the extreme sickness that was at times debilitating to her. She never dreaded being pregnant but she had to work really hard to prepare her mind for the sickness, as it lasted all day every day until the day that the baby was born.

Jada Ruth Frizzelle was born on August 10, 2009. She was perfectly healthy in every way. We are reminded daily that she is not just a blessing and addition to the family, but she truly is a promise. God taught us something that we will never forget. It is found in the story (Job 1:21 NKJV) of a man named Job: **"And he said: 'Naked I came from my mother's womb, And naked shall I return there. The Lord gave, and the Lord has taken away; Blessed be the name of the Lord.'"** God has every detail in order, both in loss and in giving in our lives, in a way that will work out for good and his purposes.

We feel like that season of our lives taught us so much about how to trust God when life's circumstances just don't make sense. Our Pastor's wife at that time, who has since passed away from cancer, would remind us all the time, "When you can't see God's hand, trust his heart."

Return to Oklahoma/More Miracles

Before returning to Oklahoma in 2010, Aaron spent time on the staff at SAGU. He was involved in recruiting and leadership areas until he accepted a call to Woodlake Assembly of God in Tulsa. He and Regan moved to Jenks, Oklahoma, with their two children, and served on staff there as lead youth pastors. We now had such a short distance to drive to see Jaxon and Jada. All of our family were now residents of and in ministry in Oklahoma. But, more miracles than we could ever imagine were still yet to come.

(As recounted by Aaron) Now comes yet another phase of miracle days for our family. Let's fast forward to a day that we really did not expect in our lives, and yet God saw it coming long before we did. We had really given up on thinking that we were going to have any more children because we were convinced that in order to have any more kids we needed some more margin in our lives and we just didn't have any. Maybe we had adopted that pressure on our own or we had adopted it from the voices that were around us. Either way, we had let that go... until 2015, when we felt like God gave us a dream that He wanted to give us another child. We had prayerfully come to the realization that our time at Woodlake Church had come to an end, and we resigned in the spring of 2015. On our final day on staff there we let everyone know that Regan was pregnant. We found out only a few weeks later that we would have another baby girl.

We really were not sure what exactly we were going to do next in ministry, but we knew that it involved loving and serving broken churches or staff teams that had served until little was left except exhaustion and burnout. What I did not know was that later that year, my father would experience one of the greatest physical battles of his entire life that would take him to the door of death and I would cover his pulpit for three months. My father, at that time, had no one that could cover for him for an extended amount of time. We had a conversation about what he was going to do… it was then that the "aha" moment clicked and I realized that resigning from my position at Woodlake Assembly had put me in perfect position to help my Dad.

(During this time, I was also enrolled at Oral Roberts University, working on my Master's Degree.) I drove from Jenks, Oklahoma, to Miami every Sunday morning, for three months straight, to preach God's word at Miami First. After service, I would head over to my Dad and Mom's house for Sunday lunch and to pray with my Dad and take a walk if he was strong enough. (Very seldom would you see yourself being placed in a position to give care to your father, still so young, yet his body wasting away.) Over those three months and the next year of his life, he got a little stronger every day. (Story told in Chapter 9, My Miracle.) To this day, we all look back at those days of suffering and yet see the miracle of God's timing in all of our footsteps and changes that set us up to walk through it together.

Regan and the kids made some of the trips to Miami with me. This pregnancy was proving to be different from her other three. She experienced some sickness in the first few weeks, but then as she was fully engaged in working on her graduate degree and fully immersed in all things pregnancy.

Regan had the best pregnancy she had ever experienced (a miracle). For any Mom that may be reading this you can imagine how much of a miracle this was. On December 14, our baby girl was born… no complications, no issues…a perfectly healthy baby. What a blessing to have children and even though they can complicate every decision of your life, especially when you have more than two, they also add a layer of joy to your life that only God can give you through your children. We named her Ivy Grace Frizzelle and her spirit has brought so much joy to our family and in our home.

Return to Texas

What we have learned from every part of this journey is how close God is, even when we can't see him, and that the pain is a part of the process to understand peace. After the birth of our daughter, Regan continued working to complete her graduate degree and to conclude her women's leadership development groups …and I searched job opportunities, checking web pages often, and continued to work on my master's degree. I had a friend who was on staff at a church in Frisco, Texas, (located in North Dallas) called Hope Fellowship. Late one night I checked their web page for job opportunities and saw a position opening for a Connections Pastor. As I read the description, not only did I feel like I would enjoy the role but I also had the qualifications. I waited about four weeks into the process and about four steps into an eighteen-step hiring process to tell my wife that we might be moving back to North Texas (which I had told her for years would happen). Four months later, I accepted the position as the Connections Pastor at the Frisco West Campus of Hope Fellowship. Little did I know or realize that eighteen months later, when the Campus Pastor left to launch a new church, I would be named the new Campus Pastor at the Frisco West Campus.

It is amazing how in both tiny steps or adjustments in our reality and in huge and unavoidable ways, God makes a way for miracles. The reason for these, I have found, are not to make us nervous about our own reality but to allow faith in Jesus to really be our Hope in the middle of a crazy reality. Aaron and Regan's house sold quickly (a miracle all in itself…) and they loaded up and moved to Texas in April 2016. They celebrated Ivy Grace's first birthday in December 2016, and remain in ministry at Hope Fellowship West Campus in Frisco, Texas.

To God be all glory for the miracle history in their family, and the miracles yet to be experienced… (miracles to be continued!).

CHAPTER 7*

Never Too Late... Miracles of Salvation

For by grace you have been saved through faith,
and that not of yourselves; it is the gift of God,
not of works, lest anyone should boast.
Ephesians 2:8-9 (NKJV)

Salvation for Regan Frizzelle's Family

My Mom's Moment (Recounted from information from Regan)

My mom started drinking at a very young age. She drank to wake up in the morning and drank to go to sleep at night. She kept a little pink glass of tequila right beside her on her desk all day long while she worked on her client's nails. My mom drank to ease the pain.

If we were to drill down into the reservoir of the ache my mom felt, we would find the level of her need for true love. My mom was never okay with not being in control; she was constantly choosing men who were insecure and immature. She did not understand her value or worth, so she was always choosing men who didn't either. It was a vicious cycle of heartbreak after heartbreak.

My mom always left us notes. We were at home a lot by ourselves because she worked long hours at her shop. She would write us notes in order to communicate with us. I remember that day well...it was a defining moment in my life, but it did not DEFINE me. I was a freshman in high school and the youngest of four kids. We were raised by a single mom, who was on the heels of her fifth failed marriage. (I have two older sisters from a different father and my brother and I have the same dad.) My oldest sister and I had gone to her shop as no one had been able to find her that day. I peeked through the front glass of her shop and read the note she had written… "I'm sorry I have disappointed you. I love each of you very much…" Reading that note felt like eternity, and I was so scared. I began to hit the glass, and yell, "MOM, MOM, open the DOOR NOW!!" After about 5 minutes of trying to get my mom's attention, and no response, my sister and I called the police.

The police arrived and moved my sister and me out of the way and got a crow bar and began to break open the door. I pushed my way through the police and began to run down the hall and around every corner. I wasn't sure what I was going to find. I rounded the last corner to find my mom sitting on the floor with an empty bottle of wild turkey and small pistol. My mom had drunk herself into a deep pit that day. She couldn't hear or see us, though her eyes were open. She sat there in silence, unaware of anything that was going on.

I was so unbelievably sad that day…my mom had never tried to give up. She had been dealt a lot of hurt in her life as well as having had a lot of blessings, but the pain of experiencing results of her decisions had brought her to her lowest moment. She had reached her pit and wanted to give up. We called the ambulance and the paramedics assisted my mom on to a stretcher. She didn't move a muscle. She was paralyzed with pain and confusion. The small glimmer of hope my mom had was gone from her in that moment. She had allowed the weight and pressures of life to sink her. As the ambulance drove off, my heart sank. What little stability I had was rolled away and was taken to a hospital in Ft. Worth.

My sister and I stayed behind and closed up her shop. My Mamaw came and picked me up and took me to the family lake house. I remember sitting on the deck with my feet in the water and feeling really depleted. I had really had enough of the chaos and was ready for something to change. I was contemplating not going back home and staying and living with my grandparents and finishing school while staying with them. Honestly, I felt really scared about the future. I had already lost touch with my dad, but losing my mom felt like a real blow to the gut. A couple of days passed and my mom called the lake house and asked for me.

The Miracle…in Motion

My mom began to tell me that she had an amazing encounter with a doctor at the hospital and he had asked if she had a Bible or went to church. Growing up we didn't own a Bible, to my knowledge, and I never saw my mom reading one. She began to tell me that God was helping her. When she came home from the hospital, she was now reading a Bible some pastor had given her. She had been praying and asking God to help her. I was very intrigued, but skeptical too.

When I hung up the phone from having the conversation with my mom, I actually felt a little change already happening. I wanted my mom to get better and I wanted to see her do it. I began to believe her and decided to go home and find out more of what she was talking about. Even though I was reluctant to totally believe any of it would last, I was hopeful that something was going to change. After that phone call with my mom, I walked out to the dock on the lake and sat down. My whole story was about to change and God was going to begin the process of bringing order and healing to my life. It was going to take a miracle from God to change our lives and my mom's life, but God was working that out. A miracle was in motion.

The woman then left her waterpot, went her way into the city, and said to the men, "Come, see a Man who told me all things that I ever did. Could this be the Christ?"
JOHN 4:28 NKJV

Going home to my mom not drinking but reading her Bible was definitely the first sign of a miracle. I was so hesitant to trust the God she had found. I was a little confused about where God had been all my life. My mom was radically changed and she began to live her faith out in front of us. All of us kids were a little apprehensive of the change. It was drastic and real and raw. She had ups and downs and still would drink a beer every now and then. She was laying down years of hard liquor so this was more than progress, this was change. She was committed to her healing and search for hope. Every day she went to work and instead of pouring her wild turkey into her pink, little glass, she poured coffee. She used to make her clients specialty liquor drinks, and now she started making fun coffee drinks and began to use her little shop after hours to do Bible studies with her clients.

My mom is a real modern-day woman at the well. The enemy lost his battle and his control the moment my mother surrendered and said "yes" to Jesus. Living almost 50 years in the slavery of sin, restoration began and the result of her redemption has changed so many lives. We all felt that this newfound faith in Jesus Christ was not going to be easy. We found opposition almost immediately. Things in our life did not change rapidly... it was a process. My mom had started following Christ and she was praying for each of her kids. We didn't grow up in church, nor did we have a Bible. The way she was living was so very foreign to all of us...it was a miracle in motion.

"My Moment"... (recounted by Regan)

My salvation came with a fight. I remember the moment as if it were yesterday. I was fourteen years old and it was Valentine's Day weekend. All my friends were going out and partying, but I decided to stay home. My mom worked eighteen hour days at the salon so I was home alone. I felt such a heaviness. I had never noticed the lingering feeling of hopelessness before, because I think when things are broken in your life and it is just survival, you don't realize you need help until it's overwhelmingly apparent that the way you have been living is just not working anymore.

I was in my room sitting on my bed and I began to feel a strong feeling of sadness. The Lies...I immediately began to have thoughts like: *"You are never going to make it in life." "Who do you think you are?" "What if people find out about your abuse?" "People are going to make fun of you at school if you read your Bible." "You can't change who you are Regan, something is wrong with you."*

I remember my mom talking to me about spiritual warfare and the devil. The warfare was going on in my mind, and I was convinced that this was the enemy. The oppression felt so strong on me. I was gripped with fear.

This was the first time I understood that the enemy was using my past against me to forge confusion in my mind, so I could not see a path to freedom. I immediately began to think thoughts that were horrible about myself. The enemy spoke intently to my weaknesses. This is what he does.

I literally felt my body shake as I cried. I felt anxious, but above all else I felt condemned and accused, as if everything in my life was my fault. I called my mom at her shop, crying hysterically. My mom got on the phone and told me to calm down. I told my mom all the thoughts that I was thinking and how I felt so discouraged and sad. What my mom did next changed everything. The hope she offered me shifted the atmosphere and calmed my spirit.

She rebuked the enemy on the phone with me. She told me that she was interceding in prayer for my salvation. The enemy was pulling out all the stops he had and did not want to lose me. My mom came home and took me on a drive. I'll never forget this drive, cruising in her white thunderbird with the sunroof down, listening to Point of Grace. I laugh now, but this was my moment.

My mom walked me through the salvation prayer and told me that as long as I trusted Jesus, there was nothing that I could ever do that would cause Him to not love me. She told me that GOD never accuses, He never lies, and He only thinks the best thoughts about us. She told me to be reminded that the enemy does not know our future. He doesn't know how or what we will choose, but that he does know the end of the Bible and he loses. He does know his time is short and he wants to take as many people with him as he can.

She told me to never give up trusting in God. God was never going to give up on me. He loved me and He was proud of me. This was the beginning of the rest of my life. I had never prayed. That Valentine's Day weekend I asked God into my heart and I have never looked back. I was eager to know Jesus. I was hungry for this HOPE. This was my TRANSFORMATION MOMENT…this was my salvation miracle.

He administers justice for the fatherless and the widow,
and loves the stranger, giving him food and clothing.
DEUTERONOMY 10:18 (NKJV)

Some people you think are just too far gone to be reached for God. This is exactly what Regan thought about her father, until God showed her differently.

My Father's Moment/(Recounted by Regan)

As I pulled up and saw him sitting on a porch of a dark vacant house (no electricity), having eaten no food for days, I thought my father was too far gone to be reached by God. However, I knew God had opened a window of time for my brother and me to rescue him. Over a plate of enchiladas, we were able to pray with my father to receive Christ and help him take the first step to committing to go to Teen challenge in Midland, Texas. Having grown up without a father and one who did not know how to care for us, I "needed" to believe in this moment…that "No one is ever too far gone for God".

In life, situations happen that we aren't prepared for and the enemy lays out schemes to take our life. My mother and father lived most of their days lost and wandering. I was an unexpected happening in their

81

life. I'm the youngest of four children from two different fathers. After my mother gave birth to her first boy, her third child, she wanted to be done having children. My dad was her second husband and my mother was becoming very unhappy in her marriage with him. After having me, my mother escaped from her marriage into the arms of her third husband, dragging us four little ones along for the ride. Like most children who come from divorced parents, I began to go back and forth between parents. My dad traveled a lot so my brother and I only got to be with him on special occasions and for a few weeks during the summer. He lived mostly with other people and in hotels until he remarried, and then he and his wife purchased a trailer. He loved his alone time where he could read the newspaper or watch TV, so when we visited, he would lock us out of the trailer house and we would play outside all day. He would put a jug of water on the porch in case we got thirsty, and to keep us from running in and out of the trailer.

He played rugby and football in college and knew a lot about sports. He completed his sophomore year in college, then got hooked on drugs and dropped out. Guilt was entangled in my father's life and played a key part in keeping him from moving forward in his relationship with us as his children. He always felt like he didn't measure up as a father and struggled with a constant feeling of insecurity. This would continue to hinder his relationship with me for years to come. What I love about our heavenly Father is that He never gives up on us. God is able to take our inadequacies and failures and use them for His glory. He never sees our lives as "leftovers". If we have breath in our lungs, God has purpose for us. He doesn't want us to think of ourselves as accidents. He doesn't throw out or waste our pain. He sees it all as beneficial to work for our good. Somewhere along the way my father believed the lie of the enemy and became discouraged by failure. People remind us of our failures, but mostly the enemy of our soul reminds us of what we will never achieve. He wants us to sit in the valley of discouragement and never reach our full potential. I have done this myself. I put my trust and weight in what people thought and it kept me from hearing what God was whispering to me. You can do the same if you're not careful. The lies of the enemy always seem loud and you feel like you can't turn the volume down. What God is saying to us is always clear, but often very soft. We can't go back and try to hear what God was trying to say to us in our moments of extreme guilt from failures, but if we can stop now and embrace the moment with God, He will prove to redeem us. My father missed those moments...maybe yours did too. We can't change what has happened to us or to our parents, but we can stop and listen and pray that God would heal our hearts and minds. We can kneel and ask for help in the midst of our greatest struggles. My mother-in-law, Cynthia Frizzelle, has always said, "Choose to do what's difficult". When we kneel and pray and ask and wait, God helps, restores and transforms. God did just that in my dad's life. At his graduation from Teen Challenge, I was totally humbled by the change in my father and proclaimed boldly to the women and daughters sitting in the audience, "Believe the best of your circumstances and trust and know that no one is ever too far gone for God."

Salvation for Laurent

A man's heart plans his ways, but the Lord directs his steps.
Proverbs 16:9 (NKJV)

Laurent's Moment

In 1994, Cynthia and I decided to sponsor a foreign exchange student through Lawton Christian School. As we looked through catalogs of young people, we decided upon a boy from Germany. We turned in our paperwork and expected to hear soon about the young man we had chosen. Sadly, we were informed that he was no longer available, so we had to go back to square one, look through catalogs of faces, and once again find the person whom we felt God wanted us to have. The moment we opened the catalog this time, our eyes were drawn to Laurent Bordin, from France. We said, "Yes! He's the one." Days of planning began to take place for us to be ready for our new "French Son", Laurent.

We welcomed Laurent with a crowd at the airport in Lawton. He spoke only a few words of English, but seemed to have such a great sense of humor, and that humor was proven when he was introduced to peanut butter. He had never eaten it, but once he tasted, he loved it with everything. His favorite sandwich was bread, mayo, bologna, peanut butter, bread REPEAT! He was sixteen years old and had no idea of what he had gotten into, but God had an appointment for him in the year to follow.

Fast forward two weeks. He was coming from a godless background into a minister's home and was to be expected to attend a Christian School. First things first, we led him to Jesus. He was so hungry, so excited to come to know the God that his new family served, "The God of the universe, who made Laurent and the entire world and his new family".

Laurent began attending class at Lawton Christian School. He also attended Lawton First Assembly church 3-4 times a week, participating in the youth group, family outings and other events. His whole life was different, and he was changed in so many ways. He was at youth group on a Wednesday night and went down to the front, telling his youth pastor that he wanted more of God. The pastor laid hands on him, and down he went on the floor. The Holy Spirit of God was doing an inner work in him there on the floor. Forty-five minutes later he stood up and all he could say was, "That was something I've never felt before."

One night at church, we had an all evening prayer night with prayer focus on requests that had been sent in from all over the world. The requests were printed on sheets of paper for people to pray over, out loud. Laurent asked Cynthia, "What do I do here"? She told him to ask God to touch, heal, provide and give a miracle to the people in need. Page after page, he went back to Cynthia and reported he had prayed for them all, and page after page, she would give him another sheet. After many sheets of praying, he returned with excitement, and told Cynthia, "I speak with another language that I don't know. What is this"? I went over to Laurent and explained to him that it was the Holy Spirit speaking through him in another language. His sincere innocence was such a joy to witness. He loved every part of coming to know Christianity.

Fast forward again. In July 2018, Laurent and his precious bride from France, Esther, came to America to visit us (his American family). We found him to be just as passionate about Jesus as ever, and Esther loved Jesus, too. They loved being here and listening and talking about all the blessings in our lives. We plan to make a trip to France in the near future, and he and Esther want to come back to America to visit us again.

We never knew when we looked through that catalog for a foreign exchange student, all that God had in store for us. Laurent laughs about the catalog story because he says we didn't choose him first, but God did! Laurent's last words after his year with us were, "I came to

America to play basketball, but God had an appointment for me at the altar".

Salvation for Cynthia's Father

...And whatever things you ask in prayer, believing, you will receive.
MATTHEW 21:22 (NKJV)

As a pastor's wife, Cynthia has taught and conducted many, many Bible study classes for women of all ages. In the spring of 2011, she taught a class on honoring those in your life. Including the teaching, she was always in personal prayer about how to honor her father, John Clements. Although he had not raised her or invested much in her life, he was her father. She so sincerely wanted to know from God how to honor those in your life that you don't spend much time with, especially a parent. One afternoon as she and I traveled to Tulsa to make a pastoral visit with someone in the hospital, God answered her question.

(Recounted by Cynthia) While traveling to Tulsa with Raymond to visit someone in the hospital, I heard an audible voice speak out loud and say, "Call your father". I was silent for a moment and began thinking to myself, I don't even know his phone number. A second time the audible voice spoke out loud, giving me his phone number. As soon as possible, I put the number in my cell phone and called. My stepmother, Jo, answered and when I asked to speak to my father, she told me he was not there, but she could put him on a three-way call. He answered and was surprised to hear my voice. I said to him, "Daddy, you know Raymond and I are pastors in Miami, Oklahoma, and we have a special Father's Day service planned this year to honor fathers". Guess what next came out of my mouth? "I would like to honor you that day". I had never been with my father on Father's Day in church in my entire life. Much to my surprise, he answered, "Yes, we will be there!" In June of 2011, Father's Day weekend, Raymond and I celebrated our thirty-fifth wedding anniversary. Our children hosted an anniversary celebration for us in the church's Connexion Center. To my surprise, again, Daddy and Jo got to be there for that occasion on Saturday, and we had family pictures taken together. This was such a special day. The big day was the next day, Father's Day 2011. I had put Daddy's picture with me at my wedding, and with all the other "father" pictures from church family, it was shown on the DVD screen that morning in church.

My sister was there also, and we all sat on the front row, together. I had not ever experienced that feeling as an adult...my Daddy with us together on a Sunday morning in church, sitting in the same row.

Raymond and I greeted the congregation and there was such a great crowd that day. I had the privilege to have my father and step-mother stand to introduce them, and I said out loud, "I would like to show honor to my father, John Clements, and his wife, Jo, today". Yes, it had come to the moment that I had asked God for over and over, "How can I honor my father that I was not raised with?" It was such a great moment, much like the feeling I had in looking down the row with my Daddy, Jo, my sister, my husband and me...all sitting there together.

Raymond preached the message that Sunday and God spoke such a powerful challenge to the men that day. The message was on purpose, purity and passion. In concluding the sermon, Pastor invited the men present to raise their hands if they were ready to have a God purpose and stay pure in their lives and have a passion to do God's will. It was a great God moment. In observing, I saw my father raise his hands. Then Pastor said to the men, "Let's take another step of faith, and if you so desire to have God purposes stay pure in your life and give your passions to God, stand to your feet". I then saw my father stand to his feet, then men all over the sanctuary began to stand. Then Pastor said, "Men, if you want to know God desires all of your life and you're willing to take all of these challenges, please join me here at the front". My father stepped away from his chair, the first person to stand at the very front where Raymond invited them to come. As Pastor began to lead the entire group of men in a prayer of commitment and surrender, I saw my father say, "I surrender". It was such an amazing moment. Everything comes into focus when you see God working with your eyes wide open. I know Daddy probably had many God moments in his seventy-six years of life, but that was a miracle and a God moment that changed everything for eternity. We had such a wonderful Father's Day and that afternoon he spoke words to me I had longed for a lifetime to hear. He looked across the table and said how proud he was of me and was so grateful to see how God had used our lives helping people. Little did we know six months later he would have a heart attack.

Called to Heaven

I got a call from my sister telling me Daddy had had a heart attack. I told her I would get on the road and be there. She told me they were probably going to release him. He had a huge blockage and the doctors were planning to deal with it through medication. I didn't go after all and sure enough he was dismissed. He wanted to be with his sweetheart, Jo, for their fiftieth wedding anniversary and take her to their favorite place. They went and when he got home, he collapsed on the floor with another heart attack. Jo called an ambulance, then she called my sister to come quickly. Daddy wanted to talk to her. He told her, "It's a big one and I love you". I was called also. Tests and studies were done over the next few days, showing there was 100% blockage, and no room for stints. He was put on a ventilator. As he came out of the procedure that checked the blockages, my sister called and put the phone up to Daddy's ear. I was crying and said to him, "Daddy, look what God has done, you have so much yet to live for," and he replied, "Honey, I'm not gonna make it, but I'll see you in heaven". It was another God moment in his life. He died on the morning of his seventy-seventh birthday. God is so good and He does things so perfect in our lives. Yes, it was all a miracle.

Salvation for Ruby

For God so loved the world that He gave His only begotten Son, that whoever believes in Him should not perish but have everlasting life.

JOHN 3:16 (NKJV)

(Recounted from information provided by Irvin Beehler) Ruby Beehler died in 2011, at 85 years old. She knew the Lord as her Savior only a short time before her death. It is never too late for the salvation experience...today, numerous years after her death, her son, Irvin Beehler, respectfully retells her story...John 3:16.

Her illness

In her late 70's, my mother became very ill. A blood clot was found in her intestines. She was referred to a doctor in Joplin, and ended up having surgery. Removal of 70% of her intestines was necessary, and we were told she would be lucky to live. She did live, and was sent to a skilled nursing facility for the care and therapy she needed for her surgery wound to heal. And it did heal and she was able to return to her home.

Her miracle

We prayed for her for years. After her recovery from surgery and healing of her wound, she continued to live in her home and we continued to pray. By now she had gotten in the habit of watching evangelists/preachers on television. One day she called and asked if we would pick her up to go to church. She attended with us that Sunday and following Sundays thereafter. On one particular Sunday, Pastor Frizzelle gave invitation for anyone who would like to be baptized to contact him to be included in the church's upcoming baptismal service. My mother responded, and she was baptized at that service. Our prayers of long standing had been answered when she accepted Jesus Christ as her Savior and gave witness in being baptized.

Never Too Late...

It was not too late for Ruby Beehler. In her eighties, she was baptized at Miami First. She received her salvation miracle...John 3:16.

SALVATION...GREATEST MIRACLE OF ALL

For by grace you have been saved through faith,
and that not of yourselves; it is the gift of God,
not of works, lest anyone should boast.
EPHESIANS 2:8-9 (NKJV)

CHAPTER 8*
Miami's Miracles

*Have I not commanded you? Be strong and of good courage;
do not be afraid, nor be dismayed,
for the Lord your God is with you wherever you go.*

JOSHUA 1:9 (NKJV)

We had known for several years that God was leading us to pastor a particular church. We had driven up to Miami, Oklahoma, to visually look at Miami First Assembly of God and walk the campus. This is yet another story to share of God's miracles working in our lives and ministry.

The Call to Miami

In 1999, Cynthia and a friend of ours who was interviewing to go to work for Teen Challenge, drove to Disney, Oklahoma, for the interview. While in this area of northeast Oklahoma, they drove by Miami

First Assembly, through Fairland and all the surrounding towns. Our friend was chosen for the position of Director for the Teen Challenge program and a short time later Cynthia and I helped her move to New Life House in Disney. We drove back through Miami and stopped at Miami First. The church secretary gave us a tour of the church and our hearts immediately knew we would be there someday.

In the summer of that year (1999) Miami First had an opening for the position of Senior Pastor. A board member from the church inquired about the possibility of me considering the position, so I sent a resume to Miami First Assembly. A group of staff and board members came to hear me speak and held an interview afterwards with Cynthia and me at a local restaurant. We felt very strongly that we would be called to Miami First. We felt so strongly that we immediately sold our house (and it sold immediately), moved into an apartment in downtown Lawton and waited on the call, but the call did not come. We found out, sometime later, the church had chosen another person to fill the vacancy of senior pastor.

During the time that followed not getting that call, God worked some amazing miracles. We continued serving in full time ministry as both children's pastors and Christian education directors at Lawton First Assembly as God began to prepare us for new areas of ministry. Cynthia was asked to be the new Director of Lawton Christian Preschool (independent of Lawton First Assembly) and I later became the associate Pastor at Lawton First Assembly. God was definitely expanding us into new areas of ministry.

During this season, Melissa graduated from college, and answered her call to go to China. We were able to get round trip tickets (gifted to us by friends) for $600.00 each that year and we spent Christmas 2001 in China and were afforded the joy of seeing the city and school where she taught. (Story told in Chapter 4 under Melissa's Call to China.) This season also brought a new member to our family. Our son, Aaron, was married in August and blessed us with our precious daughter-in-law, Regan. (Their story told in Chapter 6.)

Another opportunity presented during this season of our lives in ministry at Lawton First Assembly. We were driven to see a house in an area where we had always desired to live but thought would never be possible due to the high cost of homes in the area. When we walked into the house Cynthia began to cry as she knew this was to be our house. God was giving us a desire of our hearts. That house was to become our home for the remainder of our time in Lawton. It was a huge blessing at a cost of $35,000 below market price. We purchased the brand-new house in Pecan Valley and moved into our "miracle" new home. God gave us something we had always desired, making the impossible possible.

At the end of 2002, three and a half years later from when I first sent my resume to Miami First Assembly of God, we were again called and asked to consider having our name submitted for consideration to be Lead Pastors at Miami First Assembly. When we were called, our hearts leaped with joy, knowing the "someday" that God had already put in our hearts to be there had come.

The Move

We made the trip to Miami, Oklahoma, and spoke at the church and were voted in on January 19, 2003, to be Lead Pastors by a great majority of 97%. Our new church family moved us to Miami through frigid snowy winter weather. We arrived safely and found warm greeting among the church people on site at our new house, complete with a hot meal and sweet fellowship of welcome. (We later learned the church had a prayer team that kept prayer vigil through the entire journey of the move.) Our first official Sunday was February 2, 2003.

These years at Miami First have been a chapter of miracles in our lives, but also one of challenges. We have watched God work many, many miracles since that beginning, and have never doubted His call to the ministry at Miami First and the mission field in Miami, Oklahoma.

Every Sunday a Miracle

Miami experienced a great change with the closing of the town/county's mainstay of their economy...the local B.F. Goodrich Tire Plant. The plant, built in 1945 and opened for production in 1946, was closed down in 1986. Many local businesses struggled; some closed their doors while others maintained with reduced profits. Unemployment went to an all-time high, and people struggled; many still struggle. (At one time records indicated 72.6% of the residents of the area lived at a poverty level or below.) Miami First Assembly maintained active ministry in the community throughout this time, and continues active in ministry and outreach to people in the area. That makes every Sunday a miracle Sunday at Miami First as the church doors open and people are welcomed in to share in worship and praise and the good news of God's word...Jesus Christ, the same yesterday, today, and forever.

The Miami Mission Field

God has partnered us with a precious and generous church family. Together, we have knocked on every door in Miami, sharing the good news of Jesus and invitation to visit the body of Christ at Miami First. What a miracle of evangelistic ministry. The outreaches of our church extend to the whole city. (A church wide prayer vigil for April 7-April

21, 2019, was launched March 24, 2019, with daily prayer focus for those in the community needing salvation.) The third Sunday of each month is set aside to baptize those children and adults (as many as 19 people have been baptized in one given Sunday) who have come forward to accept Jesus Christ as Savior...the greatest miracle of all. (Salvations average over three hundred a year through Miami First's church wide and outreach ministries.)

Miami First Assembly's Family Life Center was dedicated in 1984, just two years before the closing of the B.F. Goodrich Plant. It was paid off in 1994, to the glory of God, just eight years after the closing of the plant. The two story Family Life Center hosted Joyful Learning Center ministry for over thirty-three years, and continues to host children's ministries activities as well as other family/community related activities and designated on site special programs/events.

Miami First's Joyful Learning Center (JLC) ministry opened in 1986, just two years after the Family Life Center was dedicated. After more than thirty-three years of childcare and ministry to area children and families, December 23, 2019, was chosen as the closing date for JLC. Through the years, JLC offered childcare, early childhood education and after school programs to families with children ages infant through fifth grade, Monday through Friday. JLC had "state of the art" classrooms with like staff and administrators. The teaching foundation was biblically based curriculum with age appropriate learning activities. God greatly blessed JLC over the years and answers to prayer were given time and time again...even when situations seemed impossible. God sent the miracles needed and all glory is given to Him.

The Connect Kids ministry, under the leadership of Miami First's children's pastors, has developed programs and outreaches for children pre-school through fifth grade on Sunday mornings and evenings, and Wednesday nights. The joy of baptizing children who accept Jesus as Savior is shared with the congregation as these precious ones are baptized in the church sanctuary baptismal tank with congregational witness. Through the years, Miami First's Children's Ministries have sponsored community wide activities during the seasons of summer, fall, Thanksgiving, Christmas, and Easter, to reach children and their families with the love of Jesus.

Prior to the addition of Miami First's Connexion Center, the Family Life Center also hosted the church's youth ministries. In 2009, the vision for the 14,000-sq. ft. Connexion Center to house the youth ministries (and other church/outreach activities) was launched. God provided a way for our Connexion Center to be built and in January 2010, the Center was completed and opened for youth services and activities.

Our Connexion Student Ministry "headquarters" from our Connexion Center under the leadership of Miami First's youth pastors. Services and classes for youth grades six through twelve are held on Sunday and Wednesday evenings. There's room for lots of fun activities and fellowship before and after services. Special activities and projects to support mission ministry/trips and youth camp over the summer are also part of the church's youth program as well as special projects targeting community outreach. Those who accept Jesus as Savior are baptized on the church campus, and welcomed to the family of God at Miami First.

During the campaign supporting the building of the Connexion Center, the vision for a building to house the church's NAME marriage counseling ministry was presented to the church deacon board. The $100,000 for this center was given in cash, so the NAME Center was constructed, debt free, and remains debt free.

The NEO N.A.M.E. (National Association of Marriage En-richment) Center, offers nouthetic (Bible-based) marriage coun-seling free of charge to married couples and couples preparing for marriage. Since its beginning in 2009, the Center has averaged 350 counseling sessions a year…numerous testimonies note the miracles God has given in marriages that have been saved…and all glory given to God.

Miami First has ongoing church wide ministries and fellowship activities throughout each month. The Family Life Center, The Con-nexion Center and campus grounds host many of these events, as well as special community outreach activities. The NAME Center is also used for small classes and meetings. The cost of constructing The Con-nexion Center facility still remains to be paid off in full and is the church's only debt. In October 2018, an anonymous donor gifted the church a Challenge for matching funds for every $100,000 given up to $300,000 during the year 2019. On December 31, 2018, the balance was $639,711.20. The $300,000 in matching funds has been received, leaving a December 2019 current balance of $156,179. We are thank-ing God and believing for the completion of the miracle to pay off this debt and fulfill the vision launched in 2009.

We give God all the glory for the miracle provision of these facil-ities in a community with such a long history of economic difficulties and family poverty. We thank God for the church family that gathers every Sunday, continues to believe in miracles, and partners with us in loving people into the kingdom of God.

Miami First has witnessed miracles throughout our church family in the lives of many people… physical/emotional/spiritual needs, fam-ily/marital issues, financial needs, and so much more… and the most important need of all…salvation. Some of these precious people have shared the stories of their miracles in written text. (Stories retold in Chapter 10.)

ARE YOU READY FOR YOUR MIRACLE?

The last chapter in this book (Chapter 11) will give you biblical instructions to start your journey.

Get Ready...Step Out...Walk on Water

CHAPTER 9*

My Miracle
(Miracles within Miracles)

*And the prayer of faith will save the sick,
and the Lord will raise him up. And if he has committed sins,
he will be forgiven.*

JAMES 5:15 (NKJV)

Missions Trip/First Signs

In early 2014, I went to Kolkata, India, on a missions trip with a group of pastors and our Oklahoma District Superintendent. We went to minister in the Huldah Buntain Mission of Mercy Outreach. We helped serve in the food line that fed hundreds of people who came through because they had no food. We ministered in the hospital, praying for the sick and destitute and spoke in services at different churches, sharing the word of God. Wherever we went we saw many

99

lives changed. We also assessed the needs of the buildings, school and hospital that the Mission of Mercy Outreach serviced.

During this trip, I began to battle nausea, vomiting and weakness. Cynthia was contacted and was told I needed to be hospitalized due to the severity of my issues. I refused admittance and believed God would once again take care of me and get me safely back to the U.S. By God's amazing grace I got past the immediate health threat and returned home. This was the beginning of the miracle that God would take me through in that season of my life. In sharing about the ministry work done through Mission of Mercy Outreach in India, Miami First raised $10,000 for mission work benefit in India (financial miracle).

Journey to Miracles

By the late summer of 2015, I knew I had some physical problems that were not going away, but never ever dreamed of what was to come before I would be well again. I was having digestive issues, vomiting frequently and experiencing too much pain. I just did not feel well at all. Both Cynthia and I kept attributing my health issues to a gall bladder problem, not thinking the problem could be related to my esophagus or stomach/hiatal hernia, for which I had taken medication for years. Finally, we made an appointment with a doctor in Tulsa to find out what was going on and what was needed to resolve all of this. The doctor ran some tests. The first sonogram showed no gall stones so he ordered a HIDA scan. That test showed my gall bladder was not working at all. I then had an Endoscopy done to check the health of my throat and esophagus since I had been vomiting so much. After the test was completed, the doctor came out and told Cynthia, "I think your husband has a tumor in his throat. Don't let him eat or drink anything and take him over to St. Francis South and they will do another test on him to see what we're looking at." When the doctor called with the test results, he told us my stomach was eighty percent herniated into my esophagus. It was diagnosed as an Esophageal Hiatal Hernia, which basically meant that my stomach had somehow traveled up through my esophagus and lodged in my chest. His comment was, "I don't know how he has been swallowing or eating." He also told us he would diligently look for a surgeon that would do the kind of surgery I needed to have. In the meantime, I was to have only liquids and no food to shrink my liver, which had become enlarged. In a short time, I was called and told pre-op was scheduled for September 30 and surgery on October 1. To stay as healthy as possible, we stayed away from crowds to avoid getting colds or the flu. On Thursday, October 1, 2015, I went in for surgery, thinking they would fix the problem and I would be well again in a short time. That didn't happen. This started a series of surgeries and hospital stays that lasted three months.

We checked in for my surgery at 7:00 AM. Before the surgery we laid hands on the doctor and prayed for wisdom for him as he performed my surgery. He told us the surgery would be about three and a half hours long, but ended up being five and a half hours long. Aaron, Regan, Doug and Melissa came and sat with Cynthia through the wait. They prayed over me, and at 8:30 AM I was taken into surgery. We knew there were many prayer warriors praying for me as well as my family through that time. Twice during the surgery, the doctor called Cynthia to let her and the kids know how things were going. After the surgery was concluded, the doctor told my family I was a very sick man and that my stomach was folded twice and turned like a cork screw and was up in my throat. He had to go up between my lungs and around my heart and move my chest wall to get to everything. He found that when he pulled my stomach down he thought it was completely gone

101

and would have to be removed as it was so dark colored and lifeless. He unfolded it and put it aside while he continued to work on my esophagus, removed my gall bladder and did some hernia repairs. The doctor told us later that to his complete astonishment when he looked at my stomach an hour and a half later the color was becoming normal and life was coming back into it. (Miracle noted!) He then was able to anchor my stomach in four places and put in a feeding tube for the purposes of helping to hold my stomach in place. I was then sent to recovery, and then on to my room where my family joined me and we were able to talk. I was tender, but did well. The next morning a lot of the tubes were taken out except the IV and I sat up and tried to eat a little broth. Those few nights in the hospital were rough, even with the pain medication. On Sunday, October 4, (only three days after that traumatic surgery) I was dismissed.

Cynthia took me straight to Aaron and Regan's home. Once there, due to the extreme discomfort of my incisions, I found I had to sleep sitting up in a chair. The next day (Monday, October 5) Cynthia and I decided I needed to be at home where I could begin to heal.

Once home, and with each passing day, my pain got worse and worse. The doctor increased my pain meds several times, but nothing helped. I began to decline in weight and health. I did not take any nourishment by mouth or feeding tube due to the pain. Within five days I lost seventeen pounds, and as Cynthia put it, "He was beginning to diminish before my eyes". I slept most of the time that first week home except for the time Cynthia woke me to give me meds and a few swallows of fluid. Cynthia called the surgeon's office numerous times, but they assured her everything was normal and it was to be expected. By October 7, we were very aware I was becoming congested. By evening of October 8 (just one week after the surgery) I was so weak

Cynthia decided to take me to the ER in Joplin. She gave them the details of my surgery and the ER decided to contact my surgeon. The CAT scan and X-ray showed I had pneumonia as well as something on my kidney and spleen. (There was little concern for what might be on the kidney/spleen.) I was also seriously dehydrated so was put on IV fluids and an antibiotic in the ER. Later that night, I was dismissed, and we headed home, thinking now I would get better. (Prayer warriors continued to cover me in prayer; we just had no idea of what all was yet to come.)

I had a rough weekend and was not doing well at all. By Tuesday evening, October 13, after days of pain, vomiting and not being able to swallow much at all, Cynthia took me to Tulsa to the ER. Melissa met us there and sat with Cynthia through some of the night. At 7:30 AM on October 14, I was taken by ambulance to the hospital in Tulsa where my surgery was done. I remained there for three days, sedated and on IV fluids only, to give my stomach a rest from everything. On October 17, I was dismissed to go home, with new instructions for my diet (very small amounts of liquid type foods, cream of wheat and cream soup). I did well, except for pain in my arm. It was red, hot and lumpy. A nurse friend of ours came over, examined my arm and told us it was a blood clot. Cynthia took me to the ER in Miami that night. A sonogram of my arm showed it was a blood clot in the location of where I had the IV with fluids and a vitamin pack for three days. Cynthia took me home and we began hot moist compresses and the antibiotic, praying this would take care of the problem. I agonized with the surgery pain as well as the pain from the blood clot and medications I was taking.

Cynthia called the surgery doctor and he told her not to give me any more antibiotics as it was upsetting my stomach. After a few more days, as the nausea and attempts to vomit continued, Cynthia called the doctor's office and I was prescribed new medications to take on a rotation basis. I also was taking Ensure through my feeding tube, but nothing stopped the dry heaves and vomiting. I was so sick and could not eat anything other than what was fed through the feeding tube or sipped from a cup, which resulted in my losing 54 pounds in 40 days.

This went on for days, and I was again, getting sicker and sicker and getting very little nourishment or fluids. We had great friends that kept check on us and helped with whatever we needed. Prayer warriors were on continual prayer vigil. Our son, Aaron, would come with his family each Sunday and preach services for me. (October had passed and November was now showing on the calendar, but leaves not yet turning.) Before returning home to Tulsa, he would walk with me around our yard, talk and pray with/for me. Both our family and our church family and friends were such a great support system…a great God blessing.

Cynthia realized I was again, getting worse and worse. One Sunday after the kids left, Cynthia talked with Melissa and her sister, and finally relented, calling the hospital to let them know we were coming back. She was told they would have a bed ready for me and to come on. We made the trip to Tulsa, once again. I was immediately given medication for nausea and started on an IV and pain medication. I was there for several days. During this hospital stay, God spoke to me at 3:00 AM one morning and He told me He was going to begin a restorative healing. That morning when Cynthia looked out the hospital room window, she noted tree leaves were beginning to change. Regan came to sit with me while Melissa took Cynthia for a drive to see the changing leaves. I was there for several days, then sent home with three new medications for digestion.

December came, and I was still very ill; we were also awaiting the birth of our seventh grandchild (miracle story told in chapter 6). Not only was I dealing with the physical aspects of all of this, but depression had set in from all the medications I was on (side effects). I was desperate to be free of the pain and thoughts and feelings that came with the depression. I told Cynthia I would rather die than live like this. I was in bed most of every twenty-four-hour day and she took care of me, always in prayer for answers. This was the scariest time of our family's lives and it was a part of our miracle that none of us had even prayed for but God had set in motion. One evening while she was working on a sewing project for some Christmas items, the Lord asked her if she was ready to let me go. She told Him absolutely, "NO!" From that moment on she began to speak life into me and had me up on my feet, moving around, seeking the restoration God had promised me that morning in the hospital at 3:00 AM.

December passed, and I was still dealing with issues from the October 1 surgery. In January, my feeding tube was removed and I tried eating select foods, but without much success. (I had been diagnosed with gastro paresis and given a pretty strict diet to follow.)

Pain continued, as did the depression, but it was March and I was back at work as much as I possibly could manage. (I turned 62 years old on March 30.)

Cynthia had to take me back to the doctor. Chicken was found in my esophagus and was removed. The doctor was concerned and suspected I would have to have my esophagus stretched in order for food to pass through. For two weeks, I was on a special soft diet, then I had another endoscopy.

Miracles Manifest

When the doctor came out to tell Cynthia about the procedure, he was excited with the results. My esophagus had opened wide and no stretching was needed, no repair was needed, no medication for hiatal hernia and I was ready for soft foods. (Miracle noted.) In addition to the healing of my stomach and esophagus and my body from the surgery and the medications, I no longer had to use asthma medication or treatments that had been a part of my life since childhood. (Miracle noted.)

On May 7, 2016, I had double hernia surgery (seven months after the first surgery and non-related to it). The surgery went well, and I recovered without any major issue. (Miracle noted.)

God saw us through the hardest year of our lives. We trusted and proclaimed healing like we never had before. October 1, 2016, marked one year since the surgery that changed our lives. I personally experienced the miracle that saved my life. I had returned to full time ministry by then, but was still very cautious about my diet and getting enough rest.

Celebrating Miracle/Happy Birthday

October 1, 2019 marked the fourth-year anniversary since that surgery. We remain in full time ministry at Miami First Assembly of God as lead pastors, and I continue as full-time pulpit pastor, preaching and teaching God's word to these wonderful precious people. I never forget, "I personally experienced that miracle that saved my life." God has not forgotten it, either. I was born March 30, 1954 and celebrated my 65th birthday on March 30, 2019.

Actually, I enjoyed numerous events with family and friends celebrating with me throughout the month of March. But nothing thrilled me more than the gift from God on March 31, 2019, when six people responded to the salvation altar call in the morning service that day. Three days later, during a phone call concerning some church business, I was again reminded that only because of that miracle that saved my life, was I still alive and still able to be in the soul winning ministry. The remark was made to me, "You know, the timing of those salvations in church Sunday was a special birthday gift to you from your Father in Heaven…." Yes, I knew that, and how awesome that God would remind me with six miracles of salvation. We believe and are certain there are more miracles to come in the remaining years of our ministry at Miami First.

There is so much more for us as a church family to witness and experience as the sovereignty of God moves at Miami First Assembly…

The Lord has done great things for us, And we are glad.
PSALMS 126:3 (NKJV)

And will continuing doing…as we keep our eyes on Jesus.

CHAPTER 10*
Witnessing/Receiving Miracles

...For with God nothing will be impossible._

LUKE 1:37 (NKJV)

No matter the miracle you are needing, God is more than able and ready to hear your cry. May these testimonies of miracles encourage your faith and prepare your heart… to receive a miracle.

Testimonies of Miracles in our Church Family

Joy Stoner: My Story/My Miracle

So Jesus said to them, *"Because of your unbelief; for assuredly, I say to you, if you have faith as a mustard seed, you will say to this mountain, 'Move from here to there,' and it will move; and nothing will be impossible for you.' "*

MATTHEW 17:20 (NKJV)

Cancer

My name is Joy Stoner. I believe in the Lord Jesus Christ with all my heart. I love Him, I trust Him, I believe in miracles and I know He heals today.

In the fall of 2002, I began to have several female issues, I thought. On October 30 of that year, I had a hysterectomy and began feeling better. After the New Year, Raymond & Cynthia Frizzelle became our new Pastors...a **miracle** for me. They were a very positive couple who loved the Lord and loved people! (This is important at this point, as you will see later how God used them to help build my faith.)

I continued to have a pain in my left side...it got so bad I had to have it checked out. My gynecologist in Joplin, (who is by the way a Christian...another **miracle**), sent me immediately to a urologist to check out what I thought was a bladder problem. After some tests, the urologist came in to discuss the results with us. He started by speaking very fast with words about different things, and the only word I heard was "cancer". He never stopped talking or took a breath. I stopped him and asked, "Did you say cancer?" He said, "Yes and we need to take your left kidney out as soon as possible"!!

My mind went a hundred miles an hour and I really didn't hear his words after that. I thought, "It can't be cancer, we don't have cancer

110

in our family, and what about Bill (my husband) and our family, and grandchildren? Who will take care of them, how will they get along without me? Almost immediately I felt the peace that passes all understanding spread all over me!!! God had given me that peace that He knew I would need to get me "up" this road of cancer! **I KNEW I WOULD BE ALRIGHT! IF GOD HEALED ME HERE ON EARTH, I WOULD BE FINE...IF HE HEALED ME BY TAKING ME TO HEAVEN...I WOULD STILL BE FINE!** I would be healed!! God loved me that much that He placed me in the palm of His hand and gave me that perfect peace. **A big miracle!**

Enter the Frizzelles. I had to have some tests run before surgery. Cynthia prayed for an angel to surround me and be with me throughout all the testing! AND God sent the kind angel by the name of "nurse Bonnie" who took my hand and said, "Honey, I will be with you all day as you go from test to test! You won't be alone and you don't have to be frightened or burdened as God will take that burden away!!" **Another awesome miracle!**

By this time the church family and many others around the United States were aware of my illness and prayers were going continually for me and our family. This was very comforting to me because there were days when I could not pray for myself and I knew that someone else was holding me up in prayers. I Praise the Lord for sending me loving and dedicated friends and church family.

Within a few days I had the surgery and the left kidney was removed. The tests came back. It was "Papillary renal cell carcinoma", an incurable type of kidney cancer. They gave me 5 years to live, at the most. The oncologist in the local hospital wanted me to start a chemo regiment immediately that would also require me staying at a local motel for two weeks. I would be extremely weak. It sounded so very tiring, so Bill and I decided to go home from the hospital and think about it.

My favorite scripture is Matthew 17:20 (See above.) Wow!! A mustard seed is very small…I can do that! I can have that much faith! PTL.

After being home from the hospital a few hours, Bill came into the bedroom and said he had found a hospital in Houston, TX, that was supposed to be the best cancer hospital in America and did I want to go? I told him I could not make that decision as I was too weak and that he would have to make the decision for me. He did. (Which is another **miracle** in itself.) I got right in! **Another miracle!!**

Bill called MD Anderson, in Houston, TX and made the appointment, got all their instructions, picked up all my medical records from the hospital, made arrangements to stay with a former associate pastor of Miami First and 10 days from the day of surgery, fixed me a bed in the back seat of the car and we took off to Texas. We had never been to Houston. God again showed us mercy as our Pastor friend gave us perfect instructions for the drive through Dallas and into Houston and to their home, where we stayed, and we made it without any problems. I consider that **another miracle**!

The next day we went to MD Anderson for a review and more testing. After a couple days of testing we met with the oncologist. He said he agreed with the original diagnosis of Papillary renal cycle carcinoma, an incurable cancer. He gave me five years survival. Well, that was good, at least I could get things in order for my husband and family before I went to see the Lord. Also, the Doctor said that it looked like I **would not need any chemo or treatment** as had been suggested. They would just "watch" the cancer! **Another miracle!!** Thank you Jesus. We would make the trip to Houston every three months for checkups for as long as necessary.

Everything was going well! Each trip to MD Anderson, we would see the doctor after all the testing and he would tell me that there were **"no changes"** in the cancer area. Praise the Lord! All is well and I was beginning to regain my strength! We made four to five trips a year to Houston, then in July of 2007, the fourth year since surgery, while seeing the doctor, I was told the cancer had metastasized to my lungs and there still was no cure for this type of cancer, but they could put me on a "trial drug" that they were researching, to see if it would be of benefit for kidney cancer patients. I agreed to be a part of the trial so that maybe the information they received from me could someday help someone else.

We received the very expensive pills and headed home. When we arrived home we immediately went to the church to see Pastor Frizzelle and have him pray over the "drugs". The staff was all there and they anointed the medicine bottle and prayed over it! Later I took my first pill. Thank you, Jesus, for being with me while I made this journey!

At this time, Miami First was having a series of services with Evangelist Jim King, whose wife God had healed after many years of praying for healing from her debilitating illness. **Another timing miracle!**

Evangelist King had made a CD of healing scriptures that they had listened to repeatedly during the day and night while his wife slept. The scriptures imbedded in her heart and mind building her faith! I purchased the CD, put them on an iPod, and listened to them day and night. I would listen to an hour of praise & worship music, then an hour of scriptures. It was just God and me communicating in our home for hours. I basically had blocked out the rest of the world.

It was a great time of fellowship with the Lord! The scriptures were in my heart!

After taking just a few pills, I found out that I was allergic to the meds and had to stop taking them. I had some terrible side effects. I was very disappointed, because I so wanted them to work! I still had work to do. I had unsaved family to pray for and rejoicing to do with them when God saved them!

Disappointed, we returned to MD Anderson for a checkup. The oncologist asked me how I was feeling. I told him, "OK". He said, "You ought to, because the tumor in your lungs has shrunk". Praise the Lord!!! **Another miracle!!** I would have to continue to return to MD Anderson every three months for them to watch the cancer, which we did. About the third trip down the doctor asked me, "How are you feeling?". I told him, "OK. I think I am gaining strength." He said, "You really ought to be…because if anyone looked at your reports that did not know your history, they would say there was no cancer there!" Praise the Lord…**for my completed total miracle!**

I asked the research oncologist at MD Anderson if the few pills I took had cured the cancer? He said, "No, you have not taken enough… **and there is still no cure for your type of cancer.**" I then asked him what he thought happened. He said, "Some people believe in a higher power!" I told him, "Praise the Lord, I do". I believe in miracles! Thank you, Jesus,!

It has been over 16 years since my journey up this road began! I am so humbled and grateful to my Lord for my healing when He died on the cross for me. But wait…He didn't die just for my healing…He died for everyone's healing.

"And His name, through faith in His name, has made this man strong, whom you see and know. Yes, the faith which comes through Him has given him this perfect soundness in the presence of you all."

Acts 3:16 (NKJV)

Darrell Vanpool: My Story/A Triage of Miracles

While I live I will praise the Lord; I will sing praises to my God while I have my being...

Psalm 146:2 (NKJV)

Cancer

In March 2009, I was referred for routine upper/lower GI testing by my VA medical provider. Being a veteran of Viet Nam with high exposure to Agent Orange, a baseline for future reference of any health-related problems needed to be established. Test results from the upper GI procedure gave a diagnosis of probable Barrett's Esophagus. A biopsy at Fayetteville, Arkansas, VA lab facility confirmed the diagnosis but suggested further study through the VA lab in Little Rock, Arkansas. I was referred to the VA hospital in Little Rock for another biopsy (June 2009). The results confirmed a diagnosis of esophageal cancer and a referral was made to the VA Thoracic Specialty Clinic. The surgeon presented the options: no surgery with a possible two-year survival, at best; with surgery, chemo, and radiation I could live five to seven years. The decision needed to be made within the next six months. Paula (my wife) and I were given some moments alone to process all that we had been told. There was a great sense of peace in that exam room and a notable absence of fear. Together we realized this was

115

a journey that had to be made; but we knew God already had the path laid out. Whatever and however, I knew I would choose to continue to praise the Lord at all times. The journey would be a hard one, but we knew death was not on God's agenda for me at this time. We were told it would take four to six months to have all the tests/results completed and reviewed that were necessary to confirm me as a candidate for the surgery and ensure I had the health to have a chance to survive the Ivor Lewis Esphagectomy surgery. We made the decision that day and told the surgeon to schedule surgery ASAP. God interventions began to manifest immediately as the process began. Appointment times became available, tests were done in God's timely fashion, other issues ruled out...and on August 28, 2009, the ten-hour surgery was performed. I entered the VA Surgical ICU on life support with a ventilator, gastric feeding tube, an IV line with many "feeds" and 24/7 watch/care. Days turned into weeks as Paula took up night time residence in a nearby hotel facility, where she stayed the six weeks we "lived" in Little Rock. During those six weeks, of which I have very little memory, I lived through multiple complications, and at three weeks post-surgery, the surgeon's prognosis was that I would probably not live. Paula and our sons were advised to make decisions for funeral home choice, etc. Paula gave them the information, telling them it would not be needed as we knew from the beginning of this journey I was not going to die. (During this time, prayer intercession was ongoing within our family and our church family, as well as with other churches and precious friends.)

The pathology report was delayed due to the Labor Day weekend that followed the surgery. Paula was finally given the results, with a copy of the report. She presented it to me weeks later when I became somewhat cognizant: cancer present/self contained; **NO CANCER**

PRESENT IN ANY OTHER AREA/NO FOLLOW UP CHE-MOTHERAPY OR RADIATION NEEDED.

The **miracle** had manifested; I had survived the surgery and was cancer free. The journey to recovery was now a priority prayer focus. On October 13, 2009, I was dismissed from the Little Rock VA hospital, still on the gastric feeding tube for hydration, nourishment and administration of medications. CT scan results showed leakage where the remaining esophagus had been attached to my stomach, which was now turned sideways and in my upper right chest cavity area. I remained in homebound care with phone contact with the VA Thoracic Specialty Clinic followed by three trips back to the Clinic for checkups, blood work and CT scans. On Dec. 9, 2009, the CT scan showed no evidence of any leakage or problem in the area of the connection of the stomach to the esophagus. The gastric feeding tube was removed, and my next appointment was eight weeks away. The **miracle** had manifested...I had survived the initial recovery, and was now on the journey to restore general health and eating/digestion with the dramatic revision in my anatomy from the surgery.

August 28, 2010, was the first anniversary from the surgery. By now I was on a diet with foods that I could swallow without difficulty and digest easily. Having survived the surgery and recovery, I was now scheduled for yearly checkups for lab work and CT scans to confirm the healing and restoration which continued. In October 2014, five years post-surgery, I returned to the Little Rock VA for my annual checkup, lab work and CT scan. I was dismissed from any more annual checkups, etc. I was told I had survived the five years of post-surgery and all tests indicated healing and restoration were complete. The **miracle** was confirmed...healed and restored. The journey was long and hard, but one we had to make. God was faithful through it all, and as He had told us, death for me through this was not on the agenda. We never cease to "Raise Hallelujahs and Praise You, Lord" for the triage of miracles that brought us through this traumatic time in our lives. I live, because He lives.

Paralysis X 4

In November 1973, I went deer hunting with a friend…a day that changed the rest of my life as well as my family's. I fell from a deer stand in a tree, and found myself sitting on the ground in terrific pain. I called to my hunting partner and he carried me to the pickup and took me to the local hospital. X-Rays revealed my lower back was broken. In a very short time, I began to lose feeling from waist to my feet, and was transferred to a Joplin hospital.

X 1

I was there for days, and remained paralyzed from the waist down. The orthopedic surgeon did not advise immediate surgery and expressed doubt that I would walk again. He kept me hospitalized in hopes my lower GI system would "wake up". For days, I remained bedfast, and waited and waited. I knew my family, friends, and churches around Miami were praying for me and my family. We were a young family of four, my wife and two sons, three and four years old, and we were in great need of prayer. God answered those prayers. My GI track did "wake up", and to the medical team's joy, my legs began to move. The orthopedic surgeon still did not recommend surgery, and in December, before Christmas that year, I was sent home, in a partial body cast and restricted from any work, allowing my back to begin to heal. God had given me a **miracle.** I walked out of the hospital and into my home in time to spend Christmas with my family.

X 2

From January 1974 to January 1978, I experienced healing in my back and was able to resume working my farm acreage and cattle business. Unfortunately, during that time I was never without pain, and realized by the fall of 1977 that the pain medication I had been taking was no longer working effectively. I soon began to notice difficulty with leg movement and walking. I returned to the orthopedic surgeon, and the testing revealed, while my back was healing, several areas of broken bone had fused into the spinal cord, pinching nerves, generating more pain, and affecting my ability to walk. By Dec. 1977, I was told surgery would be necessary, or I would become completely paralyzed. In January 1978, I had back surgery. Again, I knew my family, friends, and churches around Miami were praying for me and my family. The eight-hour surgery involved both the orthopedic surgeon and a neurosurgeon. Harrington steel rods were implanted in my back and I remained in the hospital until I could walk safely and pain management was adequate for me to go home. Again, I knew the **miracle** of being able to feel my legs and walk. Over the years we have had numerous opportunities to share this story, with both believers and non-believers.

X3

On Father's Day, June 15, 2008, we came home from church, had lunch, and prepared for a restful Sunday afternoon. I began to feel heat and pain in my left knee and by late afternoon we were on our way to the emergency room. Testing and blood work revealed a severe infection in my left knee, and I was hospitalized with a diagnosis of a sepsis infection. Family was notified and emergency prayer alert was sent out. Pastor Frizzelle came and prayed over me, antibiotics were started, pain medication given, and I was set for the night, expecting some relief by morning. The relief did not happen and throughout the next few days, my knee pain worsened and the infection increased. On Friday I was transferred by ambulance to a Tulsa hospital, and admitted to the critical care unit. Disease control was called in on my case. Days turned into weeks, and I could no longer walk and the pain in my knee continued to rage. I was on a broad spectrum of potent antibiotics, as lab result were inclusive as to identifying the type of infection I had. Paula was able to get a room in the hospital area available for overnight lodging. She stayed there for the six weeks we "lived" in Tulsa. The disease control doctor came in daily to check on me. He finally told me identifying the type of infection was not going to be possible and that the cause would be stated as "unknown". To add to the unknown status, were the facts that there was no injury to the knee or broken skin or any prior problem with the knee or anything present to suggest how or why this had happened. It just happened on that Father's Day Sunday afternoon. I was feeling fine, and in moments, I went down...like an attack out of nowhere.

During those six weeks, I was in physical therapy, often several times a day. The medical team was concerned as to whether I would be able to walk on that leg again. For weeks, I worked in physical therapy, and followed through with exercises in my room. By the fifth week, the infection level began to drop, and plans were made to send me home at the end of the sixth week, in a wheelchair if necessary, and continue physical therapy through a local agency. Paula and I knew I would walk again, we just didn't know how it would happen. I knew my family, my church family, friends and churches around Miami were praying for me. During the last week of my stay in the critical care facility, my leg gained strength, and with help, I was able to walk. The medical team was amazed and we left no doubt with them as to the source of my healing. I was dismissed to go home, but had to continue physical therapy locally. When we got home, and with cane support, I walked from our car to the house. Again, a **miracle**. I had "right" feeling in my leg and knee and I walked into my home.

X 4

Over the years, my back pain began to worsen. As I had exhausted pain management through injections and other options I had been given, I was referred to a pain management doctor and determined to be eligible for neurostimulator spinal cord implant to help with my pain management. On November 13, 2013, the procedure was accomplished and I was preparing to go home. Then something happened, and within thirty minutes, I was in severe pain and paralyzed from the waist down. An emergency CT scan revealed an eighteen-inch hematoma had formed on my spinal cord in my upper back. The emergency surgical team was called in (and our emergency prayer team was put on pray alert) and at 3:00 AM on November 14, 2013, surgery was performed and the hematoma was successfully removed. The damage was traumatic, and after the surgery, Paula was told I would live, but chances of my walking again were against all odds. I remained in ICU for five days, then moved to a private room. The incision area on my back was healing, and physical therapy began. However, there were no signs that I would ever walk again. I was referred to a rehabilitation facility, and we soon learned their goal was to teach me to be a well-functioning paraplegic. We requested reevaluation and a transfer to some other facility. Then the God moment happened. Our son, who is a pastor, daughter-in-law, and our almost four-year-old grandson were visiting with us in the facility. As always, just before leaving, they gathered around me, held hands, and prayed. As our son began prayer, our little grandson stopped him and said, "Dad, I want to pray first." And so he did pray a precious sweet prayer of a little child. Our son concluded in prayer and then it happened. Movement began in my right foot! Shouts of praise went up as tears flowed. We felt God's presence and the reminder that I would walk again. On December 3, 2013, I was transferred to a skilled nursing facility with a top rate physical therapist. Paula and I talked with her several times about our beliefs in God and miracles and His healing powers. She readily received us and stated she believed in God and miracles and believed I could walk again. She pledged to work with me for that to happen. Days, weeks, months slowly went by as physical therapy continued for six days a week. On March 15, 2014, with my physical therapist by my side, and Paula waiting at the car, I walked out of that nursing facility, got into our car, and we drove home. Four months and two days to the date from the day I became paralyzed the **miracle** had manifested.

I remained in physical therapy in the same facility where the surgeon that had removed the hematoma had his office. I never had an appointment with him that he did not acclaim the miracle of my being able to walk again. He had no doubt and readily gave God the praise. Through all of those weeks and months, the pain management doctor saw me numerous times, and stood in awe that not only had I not sued him, but that we welcomed him every time he came to see me. To add to our joy, he came to know the Lord in a revelation experience and was baptized by our son on June 29, 2014. We remain friends to this day, and he continues to grow and mature in the Lord. We also remain friends with my physical therapist, and she too continues to grow and mature in the Lord. We love them both and neither of them has any doubt that they witnessed a true miracle. And me, I continue "walking on the water, eyes on Jesus," knowing I live because He lives.

Paula Vanpool: My Story/My Miracle

You will keep him in perfect peace, Whose mind is stayed on You, Because he trusts in You...

ISAIAH 26:3 (NKJV)

The Facts

Due to some medical issues I was experiencing, I was referred to a neurologist and my first appointment was set for January 2012. Unable to discern the cause of the issues after examination and review of my medical history, the neurologist ordered an MRI on my brain. When he reviewed the results with me at my next appointment, I sat in shock and simply commented to him, "Really?" He told me the only concern of consequence was a lesion showing on the brain. He stated I would need to see a neurosurgeon for further diagnosis/treatment. The appointment was made, and in March 2012, my husband and I stepped into the office of this neurosurgeon, absent of fear, but wondering what was ahead and how God would show in this.

The doctor was very personable, invited us to sit down, and began the review of the "slices of my brain" that were taken during the MRI. Concluding the review, he stated that the lesion was an old one, maybe even present since birth. He suggested no treatment action, but scheduled another MRI in three months to see if any growth or change could be noted. The second MRI was scheduled for May, 2012.

On that day in May 2012, we were again in the neurosurgeon's office, waiting to learn the results of my most recent brain MRI. He again greeted us cordially, then proceeded to give us the information. No change showed on the recent MRI. Again, he recommended no treatment, but noted it needed to be watched. He suggested a follow-up MRI at some future time, with return sooner if any problems presented. We left his office, still mystified, but in perfect peace. We prayed about this for several days, and determined to leave it with the Lord, and proceed with life, with no discernment or understanding of how this would resolve, except God. Any time I would think about this, the Holy Spirit would simply remind me resolve was with God, and to just be at peace about it and give thanks. And that is what I did.

Due to some physical therapy I needed to have concerning balance issues, I was referred to my primary care giver to schedule a brain MRI to make sure there had been no change. The MRI was done on April 17, 2017, and an appointment was scheduled the following week with my doctor to review the results. This appointment I will never forget.

The Miracle

When my doctor entered the exam room, he looked at me and commented, "You have been healed. There is no brain lesion and no evidence one was ever there. The Holy Spirit has visited you." He then gave me copy of the MRI results, and the facts presented for themselves. God delivered a **miracle,** it showed on paper, and is on record in my health history for the rest of my life. Whatever happened, how it happened, when it happened, I will never know. It is only important that I know this: within my head, on my brain, I have the mark of a miracle, and the facts prove it.

And to God, be all the glory, laud, and honor...

Keisa Billings: My Story/My Miracle(s)

...Weeping may endure for a night,
But joy comes in the morning.
PSALMS 30:5(NKJV)

The beginning

"You have infertility issues." These are never words that a couple wanting to have children wants to hear. But there we were, sitting in the doctor's office, being told that it would be a long road for us to be able to have children, but with today's medicine and procedures, it was possible. Many tears were shed and many prayers went up as we began taking medication for infertility.

Several months later, God blessed us with a pregnancy with our baby's due date of August 15, 2006. We were beyond excited! My husband and I began to prepare for the birth of our first child whom we were naming Darrell James Billings, after both of our fathers. Everything was going great and we were nearing the end of the pregnancy. On August 1, 2006, we went to my doctor's appointment, excited to see our son on ultrasound and hear his heartbeat, as we had so many times during those last eight and a half months. As a mother, hearing the heartbeat of your unborn child has got to be the most beautiful sound in the world! But today, we didn't hear a heartbeat or see our son moving around and our doctor's face said it all as he got pale in the face and said that he would be right back. When he left the room, we knew something was wrong, but we didn't know what. He returned with one of the other doctors. He placed the ultrasound on my stomach, looked around for a moment and turned and said, "This baby is dead". Tears filled my eyes as I questioned him, "You're kidding, right? Everything's fine, right?" Unfortunately, the answer was still, "This baby is dead". A parent's worst nightmare was now our reality. What we had longed for and prayed for was instantly taken from us. We called family and friends to tell them the shocking news as we tried to prepare ourselves to go to the hospital to have my labor induced that evening.

On August 2, 2006, our baby boy was silently born. It was by far the hardest thing we have ever been through. Recovering from a delivery is hard enough, but adding the grief of losing your baby makes it even more difficult. I remember feeling like my heart was literally going to break into. I couldn't take a deep breath and it felt like a truck was sitting on my chest. I never really understood what people meant when they said "heartache" until this time in our lives. I really thought I was going to die myself from the grief. Sleep didn't come easily as our whole world was turned upside down. One night, as I was lying in the recliner, staring into the darkness, I saw a vision. I saw a baby girl with long dark hair crawling towards me. I knew in my heart that this was God showing me the future and His promise to me that I would have children of my own someday and He would grant me the desires of my heart. One of the verses that I held onto was Psalms 30:5, *Weeping may tarry for the night, but joy comes in the morning.* It probably wasn't going to be any morning soon, but I knew one day, "Joy" would come.

Our sons

Skip ahead several months as we began to try to get pregnant again. We knew from before that it was not going to be easy. My infertility issues had only gotten worse and we were faced with even more challenges to get pregnant. The medication wasn't working and we ended up going to an infertility specialist to discuss our options. After many different medications, treatments, and procedures, we were told that we would need to have a procedure called "in vitro fertilization" to even have a chance to have another baby. This is an extremely expensive process and with my husband being in medical school, we had no idea how we were financially going to be able to do this. We prayed that if this was the procedure for us that God would make a way. Therefore, by the grace of God, we were able to get a loan to help us pay for the procedure. I'm not going to go into all the details of the whole process for "in vitro fertilization" however, I will tell you that it is multiple steps over several weeks and each step has to go right in order to continue. On my first attempt, the medication that I had to take did not work so we had to stop. After waiting several more months, we were able to get back on the medication and start the process again. This time God blessed us with a pregnancy. We were so excited to finally be pregnant again.

This pregnancy was a challenge emotionally, because the enemy would constantly remind me of what happened last time and the fear of losing this baby would creep in. "But God!" Many prayers were going up on our behalf for a healthy baby. God was faithful to his promises, and on September 26, 2008, Jaxson Tyler was born. He was the most perfect **miracle** baby! A few months after Jaxson was born we decided to start trying again since getting pregnant was so complicated for us. I went back on the medication that we took to get pregnant with Baby DJ and in just a few short months God blessed us with a pregnancy! On July 26, 2010, our little **miracle**, Cooper Josiah, was born. God is so good! We then decided our family was complete!

Our daughter

However, I always wanted a little girl and that desire was still in my heart even though we had decided we were done having kids. A couple of years later I woke up one morning and felt just awful. My husband had been sick a couple days before so I just assumed that he had given me his sickness. But when I told him I was feeling nauseous, the first thing he said was, "Maybe you're pregnant". Knowing how much trouble we had getting pregnant with our boys, I jokingly said, "Yeah right, that would be a miracle". A few days later I was still feeling sick so I decided to take a pregnancy test before making a doctor's appointment and to my surprise it was positive! I had gotten pregnant with no medication and no prior planning on our part. However, God had other plans! Now if you will remember my vision right after Baby DJ was born, it was a little girl that He showed me. I prayed that this baby would be the baby girl that was in my vision. On December 15, 2013, God gave me the desires of my heart when our daughter, Abigail Rose, was born. She was truly a **miracle** from heaven!

I am a firm believer that everything happens for a reason and even though we didn't understand the reason during our sorrowful time, we knew that God had a plan and He was in control. At the time we lost Baby DJ, my husband was in medical school and was trying to decide which field of medicine to choose. He had narrowed it down to Obstetrics and Gynecology or Family Medicine. After we lost Baby DJ, he felt lead to go into Obstetrics and Gynecology. I know God had His hands upon this decision as Dr. Billings has been able to help several other couples who have had to go through the loss of a baby. I have also been able to help support the grieving families through prayer, words of encouragement, and even photographing their precious angel babies.

Looking back at our journey stirs so many emotions. To be honest, there were times throughout this journey that I felt like God had forsaken me, but I kept the faith and with the prayers of our family and friends, we came out victorious! God blessed us with three miracle children. "Three Miracle Babies"! Our family was now complete.

Pam Johnston: My Story/My Miracle

He sent His word and healed them,
And delivered them from their destructions.

PSALM 107:20 (NKJV)

Fevers of Death

I became ill with a high fever and very bad headache in March of 2006. At the same time, I also discovered a bite on the back of my head and neck along the mid-hairline area. I went to Freeman Urgent Care, and suspecting a possible spider bite, the doctor on duty gave me an antibiotic and sent me home. I was not feeling better after five days, and with a persistent high fever that would not break, I went back to Freeman Urgent Care. The doctor on duty this time diagnosed me with a tick bite. He changed my antibiotic and sent me home. Another five days passed, and I still did not feel better. My fever continued spiking very high, never breaking. Blood spots began to break out all over my body. My Dad and Mom came over on a Monday morning to check on me, and after seeing how sick I was, discussed it with Johnny (my husband), and they took me to the ER at Freeman hospital. I remember walking into the ER, sitting down for them to take my blood pressure and the nurse remarking that I was possibly going into shock. I remember nothing more after that until sometime Thursday afternoon. The rest of the story I learned from others. I did wake up at some point, but didn't recognize family or friends. It was a very scary time for us!

To compound things further, the doctors really didn't have answers. I had a CAT scan done and results showed that my liver was very much enlarged and blood tests showed my liver enzymes were off the charts. Johnny told them that I had been in Puerto Rico recently, visiting our daughter, and while there was bitten by a mosquito (on my arm). The doctors then also checked for possibility of Dengue Fever and gave me an antibiotic that treated a wide spectrum of diseases. On Thursday, I began to respond to the treatment and was sent home with more antibiotics. I was very weak and worked only half days for several weeks.

Shortly after I returned to work half days, I got a call from the Oklahoma State Health Department. After a forty-five-minute interview, I was informed that I had tested positive for Rocky Mountain Spotted Fever! I was shocked. I called the doctor's office to find out why no one had contacted me with this information. I was told not only that the ball been dropped but that on my chart the possibility of Dengue Fever was also noted. While the symptoms are very similar, treating one does not affect the other, as Rocky Mountain Spotted Fever is bacterial and Dengue Fever is viral. Given the length of time I was ill, the very high fever I ran, the liver issues, and the blood spots all over my body, I was told I probably had suffered from both. The antibiotics given would have helped treat the bacterial infection of the Rocky Mountain Spotted Fever, but the viral infection of the Dengue Fever just had to run its course. It was actually three months before I began to feel somewhat normal again, and nine months before I had an appetite. Some foods (mainly meats) still don't taste the same to me as they did before this illness.

In addition to being sick for so long with something I had never had before, I was subject to having people share their horror stories (or someone else's) about being sick with Rocky Mountain Spotted Fever or making scary comments about what all could happen to a person's brain who had high fevers, or discouraging tales of issues resulting from an unhealthy liver. I could not let any of that get into my mind or imagination to do battle with, so with every negative comment, I would say a prayer under my breath that I rejected that report in Jesus' name and I proclaimed, "I am healed by the blood of Jesus Christ, my Savior!".

Healing Manifested

I have had no recurring symptoms or any issues from having had Rocky Mountain Spotted Fever or Dengue Fever **(my miracle)**. I give praise to my Savior and Lord, and thanksgiving to God for those that held me up in prayer for healing from those "Fevers of Death."

Barbara Stoner: My Story/My Miracle

O God, You are my God; Early will I seek You;
My soul thirsts for You; My flesh longs for You
In a dry and thirsty land Where there is no water.

So I have looked for You in the sanctuary,
To see Your power and Your glory.

Because Your loving kindness is better than life,
My lips shall praise You. Thus I will bless You while I live;
I will lift up my hands in Your name.

My soul shall be satisfied as with marrow and fatness,
And my mouth shall praise You with joyful lips.

When I remember You on my bed,

I meditate on You in the night watches.
Because You have been my help,
Therefore in the shadow of Your wings I will rejoice.
Psalm 63:1-7 (NKJV)

An Epiphany

During late summer of 2015, I had an epiphany from God. I was sitting on the couch and all of a sudden realized if I did not get up and get my body to moving, I was going to die. I had just come through months of respiratory problems, one after another, which left me feeling very fatigued and with no energy, whatsoever. All I could accomplish in a day was my housework and fixing lunch for my husband and brother. I remember wishing they would hurry and go back to work so I could lie down. I was so tired.

During this same time I saw my granddaughters and thought they looked so good. I asked them what they were doing to look this way and they informed me that they were working with a trainer. In a few days, I caught myself wondering if that trainer would work with me to help me get up from the couch. I had my granddaughters ask her if she would work with older people. They asked their trainer and she agreed that she would work with me.

Charles and I met the trainer in Tulsa. She said she would gladly work with us to lose weight and exercise. She met with us later and taught us what exercises to do, and told us she was going to change our way of eating. This change in eating was not going to be a diet; it was going to be a life change. She had us walk two miles in thirty minutes every day and after the walk we had exercises to do.

Charles and I were dedicated to our new way of life. If we had a very busy day that did not include time for our walk and exercises, we would get up at 4:30 AM and get it done. Much to our amazement, we really enjoyed our time of exercising. As far as our new way of eating, it took a while to get used to, and for the first time in my life, I did not eat anything sweet for six weeks. We began to feel better and lose weight.

About five or six weeks into our exercise program, while we were walking, I began to get this terrible pain in the back of my throat. I kept walking and the pain went away. I talked to our trainer about it and she advised we not walk when it was cold outside. She also suggested I see my doctor.

I did not go to my doctor. In a few weeks I saw a friend who trains in cross-fit exercising. I told her about the pain in my throat when I walked. She said she had experienced the same thing and it was probably exercised induced asthma. She also suggested that I see my doctor.

Finally, I went to the doctor. When I told him about the throat pain while walking, I remember the exact words he said, "I do not know what is causing the pain so I am going to start with cardiac." He said he would schedule a stress test for me and told me to stop exercising. I did not stop exercising immediately because I did not want to stop feeling so well. After a few days, while warming up before exercising, here came the pain in my throat again. I knew I had some kind of a problem, so I stopped the exercising.

The stress test was scheduled for December 31, 2015. Stress test day arrived and after walking for two minutes and nine seconds, the pain in my throat started. The nurse had me lie down and gave me a nitroglycerin tablet (my first) and then went running down the hallway to get the doctor. When the doctor arrived, he told me I had a blockage problem and wanted me to go to the hospital that day and prepare for a cardiac catheterization the next day, January 1, 2016. I asked the doctor if he was sure I had a problem and he said that he was 99% sure. I also told him I could not go to the hospital that day because I had promised to keep my grandchildren since it was New Year's Eve. I also told him I did not want the catheterization on January 1, because everyone would be tired from the New Year's Eve celebrations.

On January 2, 2016, I was to check into Freeman hospital and the catheterization was scheduled for the next day. The morning of January 2, as we were preparing to go to the hospital, I told my husband we needed to have a talk. I told him I knew that things could happen when your heart had issues, and I wanted him to know I had no fear and I was ready to go if I did not make it through the procedure.

On January 3, I had the cardiac catheterization and made it through the procedure. The first thing the nurse told me when I arrived back in my room was, "Mrs. Barbara Stoner, God is not finished with you yet. Your LAD artery was 99% blocked". I later learned that the LAD artery supplies the blood to the left side of the heart and is often referred to as the "widow-maker infarction" due to the high death risk involved. Most people do not survive this blockage problem. God had spared my life (my **miracle**). I was glad I had that God-given epiphany on that late summer day.

Max Wagoner: My Story/My Miracle(s)

My son, give attention to my words; Incline your ear to my sayings. Do not let them depart from your eyes; Keep them in the midst of your heart; For they are life to those who find them, And health to all their flesh. Keep your heart with all diligence, For out of it spring the issues of life.

PROVERBS 4:20-23 (NKJV)

Cancer

My first experience with cancer occurred in November of 1990. I was working in Springfield, Missouri, driving from Miami each day. I started having back and hip pains and they got worse with time. I blamed it on the excessive driving. In December 1989, I was given an opportunity to retire, so I did. Unfortunately, the pains continued and I was unable to find knowledgeable medical help. In April of 1990, I developed neuropathy in both legs and feet. For the next six months, as I continued to seek help, I gradually lost weight and strength. By October, I was down to one hundred and twenty pounds and spending my days either in bed or on the couch.

Finally, I found a doctor in a Springfield clinic who had done his residency at the Mayo Clinic in Rochester, Minnesota. He pulled some strings and scheduled me an appointment with one of his classmates who was on staff. I spent two weeks undergoing tests. One of the last tests was a biopsy of a lesion on my right leg. After the biopsy, and while still in recovery, I was told a cause was found and that it was treatable. The diagnosis was "POEMS Syndrome". (The bone cancer in this Syndrome is "Osteosclerotic myeloma".) We were overjoyed with the positive news and returned home with a plan. I was able to receive radiation therapy (with no chemotherapy) in Joplin's St. John's Hospital.

My next experience was kidney cancer. In May 2009, the cancer was surgically removed. No radiation or chemotherapy was needed.

In 2013, POEMS Syndrome appeared once again, manifesting itself in both shoulders. I received radiation therapy at the Freeman Cancer Center.

Holy Spirit and Miracle (X 2)

In the fall of 2015, my doctor detected what he believed to be another Osteosclerotic lesion. We went back to Rochester. The Mayo Clinic confirmed the biopsy showed evidence of POEMS Syndrome. In his follow-up, the doctor was unable to replicate his previous results. It is my belief that I was touched by the HOLY SPIRIT on the return from Rochester.

In August of 2017, a lesion from my tongue was removed by an ENT doctor. Concerned about the remaining throat, he ordered a CAT scan. The report indicated my throat contained characteristics of cancerous tissue, necessitating closer examination. On the day scheduled for the closer examination, we made a stop so Mary Jane could grab a needed item. As I sat in the car waiting, I suddenly felt a warm feeling possess my whole body. I've never experienced this feeling before. Later in the doctor's office, while poking the long tube with the camera down me, he was commenting how clean and normal everything looked. It was then that I knew what the warm feeling was about. I am healed and cancer free...my **miracles**.

Mary Jane Barker: My story/My Miracle(s)

Therefore do not be like them. For your Father knows the things you have need of before you ask Him.

MATTHEW 6:8

In An Instant

It was Christmas break and my husband Rusty hadn't been feeling well. He had a constant cough and congestion. He had been to the doctor and had taken many different medications. It was the night before we were to return to school for the second semester and I was trying to get a decent night's sleep, because I knew the first day back at school with students would be exhausting. Rusty began feeling much worse after midnight. He had our daughters, who were home from college, take him to the ER. I knew I had to go to my school the next morning to prepare substitute plans before I could go to the hospital. I arrived at school early to get my work done. I talked to my girls on the phone and they informed me that Rusty had the flu and pneumonia. They also said the emergency room had given him too much albuterol and caused his heart to go into atrial fibrillation. This resulted in him being moved into the intensive care unit. I feverishly put my plans together and headed to the hospital. When I walked into the room, I could see the exhaustion on our daughters' faces from being up all night. Before they left to go home and get rest, I suggested we all hold hands and pray that Rusty's heart would go back into rhythm. The second our prayer ended the doctor walked into the room, looked at the monitor and said, "You just went back into sinus rhythm (normal heart rate)"! The look on our daughters' faces were of sheer amazement. I glanced down at my husband as tears filled his eyes. I remember proclaiming to the doctor and everyone else in the room, "It's a **miracle**"!

God has been so faithful in my life. I have witnessed many of His wondrous works but had never seen an instant miracle. I did that day, and it was given to my husband.

Plant The Seed

Our daughter, Hannah, suffered greatly with migraine headaches in her last years of high school. Days turned into weeks and weeks turned into months as we reached out to different doctors and specialists. We made numerous trips and had many neurology visits and surgeries. All of the medical bills were not only exhausting, but financially becoming a burden. I remember sitting in church one Sunday morning. Pastor Frizzelle always emphasized, "Plant the seed, expect the harvest". I remember looking into my purse as the offering plate began moving down the aisle. I had only one dollar bill in my purse. I knew it wasn't much, but I remember saying, "God bless this offering".

I began the new work week not even thinking about the dollar I had put in the offering. However, much to our surprise, we were blessed with an unexpected check of $2,400. I instantly thought about the only dollar I had in my purse and how God had turned it into a **miracle.** He knows what we have need of and never fails to provide for us, in His timing.

Liz Doty: My Story/My Miracle

The Lord will fight for you, and you shall hold your peace.
Exodus 14:14 (NKJV)

The Birth

Elliott, our first child, was born on April 21, 2016. From the time, I was thirty-one weeks pregnant with him, I had to have fluid removed every other week due to the high fluid levels I experienced. On April 21, I kept my regular appointment to have fluid drawn. Elliot's heart rate was lower than normal, but not low enough to be concerning to the doctors. They proceeded with the fluid draw. It took close to an hour and a half to take off several liters of fluid. At the end of the draw, the doctors checked Elliott's heart rate and it had dropped to 93. They immediately went into panic mode and told Alan and me to go directly to the hospital. We were told that Elliott would need to be delivered by emergency c-section. When we got to the hospital, they quickly hooked me up to the monitors. Elliott's heart rate had gone back up to 120-130 range. They monitored him while my doctor and the specialist that had done the fluid draw discussed the best course of procedure to deliver Elliott.

It was decided that a c-section was necessary, so they prepped me and I walked from the delivery room to the operating room. I was given a spinal block and waited for Elliott's heartbeat to show on the monitor. They searched for it, but no heartbeat showed. Alan was brought in and delivery began. After what seemed like an eternity, the doctor told Alan and me that Elliott was really struggling, and we needed to pray. Alan and I began praying. A delivery nurse came to my head, laid her hands on me and began praying also. The doctor said that Elliott wasn't doing well at all, and that she was going to pray. She began to pray out loud in the delivery room. We had no idea at that point that our precious baby boy had been born dead. Miraculously, after six minutes with no heartbeat or breathing, he began to breathe and his heart started beating.

NICU

Elliott was immediately taken out of the delivery room by the NICU team and put on a ventilator. I remember them stopping so that I could see him for a split second. His eyes were dark and he had a ton of hair. He looked just like his daddy. I had no idea at that point that my sweet boy had a very long, hard road ahead. He was taken to NICU, and I was taken to recovery.

When my doctor and the NICU team came to the recovery room they told us that the next seventy-two hours would be very critical for Elliott. They explained that when the body goes that long without oxygen it begins the process of shutting down all of the organs with an acid. They explained that he could have severe brain trauma and a "laundry list" of things that could be wrong. They also explained that he would be on "body cooling" for the next seventy-two hours, and that during that time he would have to remain on the ventilator and would be sedated, with a body temperature of 87 degrees. This process would help prevent further brain damage and hopefully help the brain heal from the trauma. They told us that at the end of those seventy-two hours we would "have some decisions to make". Later that evening, the NICU ran an EEG on Elliott and came to my room to tell us that the EEG showed abnormal brain activity. We were told that could mean a variety of things, including seizures, but at this time they could not clarify exactly what his abnormal brain activity would be. The next seventy-two hours seemed like time just stood still, and we didn't know what the future held for our precious baby. One promising thing did happen during that time as Elliott was taken off the ventilator and was able to be put on a bubbling C-pap machine. Thankfully, at the end of the three days, Elliott was warmed back to normal body temperature and brought out of the sedation. While things looked promising, he had a lot of difficulty breathing on his own with the C-pap machine. He was at 80% oxygen and struggling to hold his stats. The NICU doctors decided to try nitric oxide. It is naturally produced in the body, but this was an extra boost of it, and should have helped Elliott in the first eight hours or so. Sadly, there was no change and Elliott continued to struggle.

The Miracle

So again we asked for prayers. In less than twenty-four hours, Elliott went from 80% oxygen on a bubbling C-pap machine to room air with no oxygen support at all. We spent seventeen days in the NICU, and before we were allowed to leave, he had an MRI done that showed NO delays or abnormal brain activity, and a second EEG that showed NO abnormal brain activity or seizure activity. Elliott left the NICU a perfectly healthy baby. We did follow up with some therapy, but the results of the last MRI and EEG evidenced the miracle that happened to our baby boy.

Today Elliott is a normal three-year-old, little boy! He talks, walks, plays, runs, and is EVERYTHING that a little boy that had his beginning shouldn't be. He is our **miracle**, and I thank God for the miracle that I get to kiss every day.

Rocky and Karra Staggs: Our Story/Our Miracle

Rest in the Lord, and wait patiently for Him...
PSALMS 37:7 (NKJV)

Married

In July 2007, Rocky and I were married. He had just turned twenty-one and I had just turned twenty-two. We both had attended NSU in Tahlequah, Oklahoma, had jobs, and were excited to start our lives together as Mr. and Mrs. Staggs. We wanted to have children, and decided to fully trust God with the growth of our family; when and how many children we would have would be up to Him.

Adoption

We celebrated our third wedding anniversary July 14, 2010, still a family of two. We loved children, and frequently did babysitting for friends of ours who were foster parents. We fell in love with one of the boys in their home. Allen is a very special child and in April, 2011, we were granted the DHS placement of this three year old boy in our home. In March of 2012, we finalized the adoption and Allen became ours. We now had a family of three, and while we experienced difficulties, we knew he had been created just for us.

Miracle Child

As the years went by, we both gained peace that Allen would be our only child. In April of 2018, we joined the staff at Miami First Assembly of God in Miami, Oklahoma, as Children's Pastors. We got off to a very busy start in children's ministries and continued that way as we planned and worked through the summer and early fall activities. Then, in November of 2018, something happened that surprised us,

142

and allowed us to surprise our family and friends. I felt a sudden strong movement in my abdomen and went to the doctor to confirm what I thought was the situation. I was not only told I was pregnant, but that I was 25 weeks into the pregnancy. We soon found out our baby was a little girl and due to be born in February. And the miracle did happen. On February 25, 2019, at 8:35 AM, Ember Grace was born into our family. God has grown us to a family of four and we give Him the glory and honor.

Janet Venegoni: My Story/My Miracle

"The eternal God is your refuge, And underneath are the everlasting arms; He will thrust out the enemy from before you And will say, 'Destroy!' "

DEUTERONOMY 33:27

The Warning

It was a morning in early October 2015. I worked as the assistant director at Joyful Learning Center daycare and generally divided my time between my desk and the building's two floors of daycare. That morning was no different. I was sitting at my desk working through daily paperwork when I suddenly felt a sharp stabbing pain in my chest and tightness that took me aback. I sank back into my chair, trying to catch my breath. "I must be having a heart attack" was the first thought that crossed my mind. Before I could think of anything else, I heard one of the teachers calling for me. She needed help with getting two toddlers back to their classroom...up a flight of stairs. I got up from my chair and walked slowly down the hallway, then up the stairs. I held on to the railing to steady myself through the pain, one excruciating step at a time. But it was no use. Once I reached a landing, I had to stop and sit down. It took a full five minutes before the pain and tightness on my chest subsided and I could catch my breath again. Once I regained my footing, I walked away from those stairs as if nothing had ever happened.

The Mass

A few days later, on October 16, I had a routine appointment with my primary care physician. I still felt fine and I almost decided against keeping the appointment. It's a good thing I have friends who strongly advised me to not ignore the experience from the few days prior. As a preventative measure, my doctor sent me for an X-ray and referred me for appointments with a cardiologist and pulmonologist. Within a few hours after my appointment, my doctor called to say that the X-ray showed a mass in my right lung and to return to the hospital that day for a CT scan. As I was out and about shuttling Joyful kiddos for a field trip day, I told her that I probably would not be able to return that same day. My doctor would not hear of that. She arranged for a CT technician to wait for me and perform the scan after hours. Her sense of urgency was quite unnerving.

A few more days transpired before it was time for my appointments with the specialty doctors. The cardiologist determined from X-ray and CT scan results that my heart was healthy, which was a relief. However, that feeling was short-lived. About twenty-four hours later, the pulmonologist told me that the only way to know exactly what was showing on the scans was to perform a biopsy and a bronchoscopy as soon as possible. Those procedures were scheduled for November 13, a Friday that I will never forget.

Following the procedures, the doctor met with my sister. I had asked her to join me on my appointments, as she had worked in medical transcription for many years and she was very comfortable speaking with medical professionals. When she relayed to me about what was said in the meeting, she said that his demeanor was somber when he first came into the room. She immediately knew what he would say… cancer.

Cancer

He explained to my sister that the mass was very large. It covered my entire lung, and even with surgery, they probably would not be able to get it all without removing the entire lung. He continued on to say that it was a very aggressive cancer and that I had six months left to live at the most. We would have to wait until the following Tuesday or Wednesday for the biopsy results to confirm his suspicions, but he clearly stated… "I know what I saw".

I spent the rest of that November day recovering from those procedures. As I lay on my couch, nauseous and tired from the anesthesia, thoughts whirled from all directions in my mind. It was overwhelming, trying to process the gravity of the doctor's words… *"Only six months left to live."* With tears flowing from my eyes, I thought of my children and my new grandson—the thought of leaving them behind hurt more than words can express. I thought of my family and of dear friends— my heart was breaking. I cried out to Jesus, right there from my couch, and His presence became very real and tangible to me at that moment. I told Him, with all of my heart, "Jesus, I am going to trust You. If You heal me of this and allow me to stay here, or if You choose to take me home, I will say yes. Whatever choice brings You the most glory, I will trust You." At that point, I felt God's peace settle over me, and I fell asleep.

Life had to continue. I had committed to drive a group of ladies to a Propel Women's Conference in Tulsa, Oklahoma, the following day. I certainly did not feel like seeing anyone, but I did not want to let those ladies down by backing out at the last minute, either. To this day, I am so very thankful that I did not let my feelings make my choice.

Prayer

The church was filled with ladies ready to worship. As Kari Jobe began to lead the worship service, the presence of the Lord seemed to wash over that room like a wave. Suddenly, Christine Caine walked onto the stage and caught Kari's attention. Kari let her voice fade out, and the musicians continued to play softly. Christine said that she had never interrupted singing like that before, but she felt the overwhelming power of God and that He was there for healing. She asked everyone who had been given an impossible diagnosis to stand. Along with others, I stood immediately. Several ladies laid hands on me and prayed. The peace of God settled down over me so completely that I knew beyond any doubt that whatever road was ahead of me, my trust was in God and everything was going to be okay.

The Miracles

On the following Monday morning, I was at work when my phone rang. It was the pulmonologist. He sounded elated as he explained that he had just spoken to the pathologist. The reports from the biopsy showed NO malignancy! I did NOT have cancer!

Since the mass was still there, the pulmonologist scheduled me for periodic follow-up CT scans and checkups. With each passing appointment, with no treatments or medication of any kind, that mass continued to shrink. On September 20, 2016, nearly one year after I

was told I had only six months to live, I was told that I no longer needed to follow up because the mass was gone! The miracle was completed.

**To God alone be the glory and praise!
He truly is my healer and the lifter of my head.**

Matt Watts: My Story/My Miracle

*There's no shadow You won't light up, mountain You won't
climb up, coming after me. There's no wall You won't kick
down, lie You won't tear down, coming after me!*
(RECKLESS LOVE – CORY ASBURY)

The healing and restoration that has taken place in my life and my
family's life cannot be completely put into words. There is no question
God is sovereign. I have experienced Him turn me around from near
death, depression, health issues, anxiety and addiction. The hardest part
for me was knowing my wife and kids were being hurt the most, without knowing the reality of what I was doing to myself and them. But,
here I am today, fully in belief that I am a child of God and I have been
healed, delivered and restored by the grace of God. This is my testimony…MY miracle!

Thyroid Cancer

I'm sure most of us could trace back personal issues and hang ups
all the way to our childhood. I know I could, but, this story starts a
couple of years ago when I learned I had thyroid cancer. My thyroid
cancer was found by a miracle all its own. I was at a routine doctor's
appointment for my heart. The doctor had read a recent CT scan of
my chest and noticed a few nodules at the very top of the scan that
turned out to be cancerous thyroid nodules. A few months later, I went

through radiation and removal of my thyroid. I thought this was the end of my problems, but the enemy had just begun.

I had known the Lord for some time before this, but I now know the devil still held some strongholds on my life ever since I can remember. As the realization of cancer set in, I couldn't help but think of my Mom. In my early 20's, my Mom passed away from battling cancer for years and I always wondered if this would be just the start of my cancer battle. After my surgery, anxiety and depression came in like a flood. I had the perfect wife and kids and a great job. I had nothing to be anxious or depressed about, right? I learned the devil will use anything, big or small, to bring a person down.

Strongholds

One of my biggest strongholds from adolescence was my illicit drug use and drinking...using, buying and selling anything I could get my hands on. After getting married and starting a family, I thought that part of me had died and I would become the perfect husband and Dad. Once again, Satan had his plans.

Back to my ever-growing depression and anxiety after the surgery, my wife would more often than not find me in bed or being extremely irritable for no reason. You would have thought I was completely helpless. My wife would do her best to accommodate my ridiculous state, even though it was driving her to tears constantly. My kids quickly began to look at me like a stranger rather than a Dad. I had gone from being extremely happy and feeling blessed for everything in my life, to feeling like getting out of bed was the most difficult challenge of my life. My mind began to start thinking of ways out, but before suicide became the first choice, I resorted to the lifeline I had always hung on to since adolescence - my hometown connections. I quickly found myself in a crippling prescription medication addiction. I was wrong in thinking that the medicine would help my problems; it only compounded my anxiety and depression. My mental stability was something I had always relied on up until then, and it was now fading fast.

The most incredible part of this testimony comes from my wife, who not only dealt with each one of these issues whether she knew about it or not, but who also prayed like never before to have this sorted out. I know in her mind she had run out of answers, and giving this to God was the only option. Going back and reading some of her written prayers is downright bone chilling! Absolutely prophetic! But once again, it was still going to get worse before it got better.

Surviving on a day to day basis was becoming harder and harder, for both my wife and me. All the things I had enjoyed in life had all gone by the wayside: hobbies, friends, family, church...all of it seemed to mean nothing anymore.

I had a job opportunity come up in my hometown and secretly knew this would allow me to be closer to my fix. Nothing was stopping me from going back to my hometown; at one point, I even left my wife alone, crying with our kids, to finish packing all our stuff. Instead of a transition to a new town for my family, my wife moved in with a family member as did I. We were separated, and I didn't seem to mind one bit. My addiction had now gone from a daily fix to an hourly fix. I was knocking on death's door multiple times a day. In fact, I would still manage to argue with my wife and tell her how this was all her fault. I hardly saw her or my kids. I left her, talking myself into thinking how she is better off without me, but where my mental toughness was now nowhere to be found, my wife prayed with a mental toughness that was anointed by God. I can promise you I have seen people divorce for just one of the issues we faced, let alone everything we were up against. I was so deep in the devil's plan that I thought I was doing all the right things.

The Lord knows me. He knew how hard my heart was to certain things in my life, in my past. I know He has been there all along, thus the restoration began. Seven months of separation and God was ready to start REALLY revealing His power to me! My wife now knew of my addiction and it had now become a matter of life and death for me. I was suicidal daily, not able to keep up with my addiction and failures.

Restoration…the beginning

One morning my wife found where I was hiding out and called me to tell me she was waiting outside. She wasn't kidding! She waited for hours. My mind raced at the thought of my wife waiting outside for me to sign divorce papers or even have me arrested, but most definitely I knew we would have more arguing. Finally, I walked to the car, preparing for the biggest argument and blow up of my life. I slowly opened the door and got in. There was complete silence. No yelling, no judging - just love. I now know the Lord was SO present in that car. There had been years of arguing, tears and questions, but in this moment, my wife ever so calmly told me she loved me and wanted to fix this. My flesh deserved to be deserted right there that morning and I promise you, before I got in that car, I had no plans of changing my course. I knew I would argue with her, most likely lose her and my kids and then get out of the car and go right back to my ways. That would have been game, set and match for Satan. I truly mean it when I say I would have been lucky to live another month. Instead, God revealed that I would soon be living like it was my first time!

Most people in my position would have had a long uphill battle to deal with as far as treating addiction, depression and anxiety. My family was ready to try any and every rehab facility and/or doctor they could find, but I know God spoke to me and told me if I would let him, He would do all that for me….and HE did. However, He didn't mind teaching me a lesson along the way.

Instead of getting out of that car and allowing the enemy his ultimate victory, I rode off with my wife, declaring I could do this with or without doctors or facilities. God was showing me the firm foundation I had all along, not only through His grace, but the foundation of my wife, my family and all the prayers that were building me up without me knowing it. It took a lot of begging, but I convinced her I could do it.

A week sober, my mental stability wasn't getting better. It was worse than ever before. I was hallucinating, along with vomiting and severe muscle cramps. The irony was that now I truly wasn't able to get out of bed and it was no laughing matter. I was supposed to get better day by day, but I was getting worse.

One morning my wife had incessantly tried to get me to respond. She tried to get me to move a finger or something, but I was unable to respond. It was worse more so than the previous days and she realized the gravity of the situation. I don't remember any of the following part of my story as I was rushed to the hospital, intubated and put in ICU. I spent five days in the hospital before a team of doctors decided not only was I healthy enough to go home, but that I was mentally stable and not going to harm myself. Before this episode, I took great pride in my mental acuity, but now I had to sit back and listen to all the stories of my hallucinations and downright craziness leading up to the time while in the hospital. All I remember is waking up in the hospital with my wife sitting at the foot of my bed smiling. I remember wondering, "Why in the world is she still here, let alone, smiling at me?". I thought she would be long gone after everything I had put her through. Thank God, I was wrong.

Leading up to my "oh so personal" encounter with God, I was down for the count. Dead. My bones were DRY. It is a 100% miracle, a wondrous act of God, that I am able to write this testimony today. I have had prayer and support my entire life, but none of it was as palpable to me as it was in this period. I am a better person than I have ever been. My whole life I have had a struggle with the enemy. I struggled to keep from going back to the person I was. The enemy wanted me back to telling myself daily that I was not good enough for anybody or anything and telling myself, as long as I keep a good poker face, that all is well and no one would figure me out.

The thief comes only to steal, kill and destroy. I came that they may have life and have it abundantly.

(John 10:10)

Full Restoration

When I finally surrendered my entire heart, then and only then was God able to start full restoration in my life. No longer did I let the enemy have the strongholds in my life that he had for so many years. He was out to kill me, but God created something beautiful out of my ashes.

To be honest, after my hospitalization, my family and I would still question the future. I've always heard God's word does not return void. I learned this truth first hand through the prayers prayed for me. With the hospital stay over and the realization that I was still alive, I now faced the future. No house. No job. More debt. Warrants. Burned bridges. Trust destroyed. A family to feed and a family I had to prove myself to all over again. These mountains I faced seemed destined to tear me down; push me back to my old ways, but God can do the impossible and He did!

Like never before, I praised His name through every step of the way, through every one of those mountains. Before I could even begin to let the anxiety that had once left me paralyzed take over my faith, God answered our prayers for our future. Within two months we relocated to another state. I had gotten a better job, with a higher salary than ever before. This allowed my wife to stay home with our kids instead of having to work. Not only did I get a better job, my hours were much less, leaving more time than ever to spend with my family. God has shown me what family really means; how to plant generational seeds in my family, for their future. We found an incredible church to get involved in and have met many new friends. He has supplied every single one of our needs and more! *And we know that in ALL things God works for the good of those who love Him, who have been called according to His purpose.* (Romans 8:28)

God healed my spirit through praise and worship, saturating my soul (I think the song, Reckless Love, was written just for me) because I was unable to concentrate and focus on reading the Bible. He truly left the 99 to find me. He knew I wanted to keep running away and He knew exactly what I needed to go through to show me His true love! *"For my thoughts are not your thoughts, neither are your ways My ways," saith the Lord.* (Isaiah 55:8 KJV) I have a true understanding of this verse now more than ever and I know I don't have to try to understand, Jesus died for ME. He gave His life so I could go through this and come out on the other side with a personal relationship with Him and an ability to share my story with others. I know I caused a lot of destruction, but the blood of Christ allows me to move forward in His love and turn this life into a life worth living. Oh…how He loves us!

It chases me down, fights 'til I'm found, leaves the ninety-nine. I couldn't earn it, I don't deserve it, still You give Yourself away. The overwhelming, never-ending, Reckless love of God.

(RECKLESS LOVE – CORY ASBURY)

Brandon and Keri Clapp: Our story/Our miracles

Though one may be overpowered by another, two can withstand him. And a threefold cord is not quickly broken.

ECCLESIASTES 4:12 (NKJV)

Marriage…a word often used without care

In April of 2013, my husband and I got married. Our wedding was simple and quick. We loved each other and felt like it was the right time to get married as we already had a daughter and were now expecting our second child. It just made sense to get married. So now the fairy tale of husband and wife things should become real, right? Life should get easier for us as a happy little family. We started living the married life and quickly realized that things were no different than before.

We still were struggling to pay bills and with a second kid it was even harder. Plus, on top of it all, we kept on fighting nonstop. We questioned why we married each other and it soon came to the point where we despised each other and looked for attention elsewhere. It didn't take long before we decided since it was just a piece of paper we signed when we got married, we could just get a divorce and that would solve all the problems we were still having. With that decision made, the next step was to tell our moms. The next week we would talk to a lawyer to figure out where to go from there. Life for both of us was miserable.

A couple of days later we got a call from Brandon's Grandma Betty. She wanted to get us an appointment at her church at their NAME Center for marriage counseling. It was free and she thought we should at least try it before getting a divorce. We said sure, but then skipped the appointment that was scheduled because we didn't see any reason to go. Grandma Betty called again and asked us to please try it, at least once, before calling it quits. Brandon and I argued about it (of course) and he told me he wanted to try the counseling so that when we did get a divorce, at least he could tell his Grandma he tried.

We showed up at the church NAME center for the next appointment. I did not want to go in at all, but we walked in and met Roger and Crystal Wynn. They were two of the marriage counselors at the NAME center. We went into a room and sat down, but didn't know what to expect. By the end of our time that first appointment, Brandon and I both left crying. We had learned so much about how marriage was suppose to work and we kept going back to our next appointments.

Salvation for Brandon and Keri

Brandon recalls that on the second appointment he decided to give his life to the Lord. I had accepted Jesus as my Savior about a year earlier in a service with Evangelist Ron Rhoads.

Married and Saved

One of the most important things we learned from marriage counseling was that marriage is a covenant and not a commitment. It's more than a piece of paper. We realized there will be good days, bad days, and hard days…and it's work. God did not say life would be easy, but He will be here for us through it all. We soon found ourselves living life with God in the center of our marriage, and the blessings started pouring in. We went from almost being evicted from our home and not knowing how we were going to pay rent and keep the lights on, to getting a check from Brandon's business for the exact amount for our rent - to the penny. You may think "coincidence", but we say only GOD. We still struggled financially, as our jobs were not enough to get us back up to the surface. However, one day we got the biggest blessing (besides our marriage being saved and our children). A wonderful lady who knew Brandon through his job and had talked to him about our house situation, came to him and told him we needed her house. She told him it was everything we needed and she was moving out of state. She informed us that it was big enough, in the school district we wanted, and in the country. Brandon told her it sounded amazing, but that we were not in the spot to buy anything right then. She said, "You don't understand what I am saying Brandon, I am wanting to give you my house." At first it just wasn't believable. I mean, who just blesses someone with a house? But the more we talked, the more she insisted she wanted to do it. She proceeded to tell us that God told her to give us her house. We graciously accepted this miracle.

Fast forward to almost 6 years later. April 13, 2019, Brandon and I will be married 6 years. We now have three children, a dog, a house, and a car. All of it is paid off. We got our license through our church's NAME Center to be marriage counselors ourselves, so we can bless other couples as we were blessed. We have been blessed with Brandon starting his own business and I got to quit my job and stay home.

Now don't misunderstand, we still have times we struggle just like everyone else and there are times we argue and disagree. However, the one thing that changed for us, better than any fairy tale, is the fact that GOD is now the center of our lives. Things break, we bruise, but nothing can take away our GOD. The devil attacks daily and some days we let him slip through the cracks, but God always comes through quickly to remind us that He is here. We are excited to see what the future holds. Yes, I may get a flat tire tomorrow or Brandon will forget to put his laundry in the hamper, but now we know how to handle things, whereas before we didn't know the power of God's Grace and Love. As Brandon says, "Don't put God in a box."

John Buxani: My Story/My Miracle

No temptation has overtaken you except such as is common to man; but God is faithful, who will not allow you to be tempted beyond what you are able, but with the temptation will also make the way of escape, that you may be able to bear it.

1 CORINTHIANS 10:13 (NKJV)

The Warning

On Thursday afternoon, June 1, 2017, I was sitting at the volunteers' desk at the hospital, when a friend of mine from our church came into the waiting room. I asked him what he was doing there and he told me he had brought his wife in for a cardiac catheterization. We then visited about the open-heart surgery he had had a couple of years prior. In describing what kind of symptoms, he experienced, he told me that he had felt congested, had a hard time breathing and had some chest pain. I thought to myself, "I had those symptoms a couple weeks ago". They did not last long, so I did not think any more about it.

At 4:25 AM the next day, Friday morning, I woke up to the same symptoms plus I was sweating profusely. I woke my wife and asked her to take me to the ER. Upon arrival, they did some blood work, an EKG and ran some other tests. Later that day, they did a cardiac catheterization and found out my "widow maker" had 99% blockage! I was taken to Freeman hospital by ambulance, and had open heart surgery the next day, Saturday morning.

The Miracle

After several days of effective pain management and healing, I was dismissed to go home. Thank you, Jesus. I know this was a miracle, because if I had not seen my friend and learned of his symptoms, I would not have been alert to what was happening, and would have just laid in bed that Friday morning and probably died. The other miracle was my healing so fast after open heart surgery.

Again…Thank You, Jesus.

Charles Stoner: My Story/My Miracle

Trust in the Lord with all your heart,
And lean not on your own understanding;
In all your ways acknowledge Him,
And He shall direct your paths.
PROVERBS 3:5-6 (NKJV)

My beginning

Looking back over my childhood, I realize at the time I did not know I was born into a poor family and that my parents faced many financial challenges. My parents may have been poor, but I always knew they loved me and they would do anything they could to help me. There was one thing for sure, God was number one in my family. I grew up helping my parents as they worked on the farm performing such duties as milking cows, feeding pigs, and farming with tractors and other farm equipment.

When I was five years old, my dad had a gallbladder operation (1945) and it didn't go well. He became very ill and it looked as if he would not survive the operation. I thought about it several times as I became older, and have always thanked God that my dad made it through that time in his life. During that time, my mother had my baby sister, Elaine, and me to care for, plus the farm. She was also my dad's caregiver as he regained his health. My grandfather, Walter Stoner, was also very good to help us during this time.

While my dad was still in the hospital, two preachers came one Sunday afternoon to pray for his healing. My dad told me later that he felt sure he was dying that day because his body was beginning to get cold, starting at his feet and progressing to just beneath his heart. That was when the two preachers prayed for him, and he said within thirty minutes his body began warming. The warm feeling started just below his heart and went all the way down to his feet. He was still not able to do much when he came home from the hospital, but he started getting better.

I attended several schools (Peoria District, Sunnyside and Oak Grove) before starting my freshman year at Quapaw High School. My first year was miserable for me, as I suffered a bad dose of bullying from four boys from Peoria. Thankfully, my sophomore year was better. Miss Madelyn Myers, my history teacher, really did a lot for my self-confidence. She and my parents had a more positive influence on my life than anyone else. She took an interest in me and always encouraged me to do the very best I could in my school work. She would say, "You never know where it will take you".

My Career

After I graduated from Quapaw High School, I attended Joplin Business College in Joplin, Missouri. I attended the business college for one year and after graduating from there with a business degree, I started looking for a job. In June 1959, I applied at the First National Bank in Miami, Oklahoma. Mr. Harold Mullendore was the Executive Vice President and he told me when he interviewed me for a job, "I knew your great grandfather, your grandfather, and your father. If you are half as good a man as they are, you will do just fine". He hired me, and I began work on July 1, 1959. My job was not a glamorous one, but I was happy to have it.

I worked in the bookkeeping department along with a large group of women. My supervisor was a really good friend to me and encouraged me to read his Institute of Banking books. As I began studying them, he told me I was the best student of banking that he had ever seen. He told me that he did not want to lose me, but he knew that I would be moving up to a better job and suggested that I try to find a small bank to work for. His theory was that in a small bank I would have to do a little bit of everything and could get the big picture of the banking business. For two years and eight months I worked at First National. I was looking for that small bank for a few months before I found an opportunity to make the job change. March 1, 1962, I began my banking career with the Welch State Bank in Welch, Oklahoma. Little did I know of the miracle God had in store for me.

I was engaged to a beautiful lady from Fairland, Oklahoma, by the name of Barbara Bland. Barbara and I were married July 21, 1962. She had applied for a teaching job in Welch Public Schools and was hired to teach English and speech.

Sowing and Reaping

As we started our life together, paying our bills was always a priority. We did fine. Then one Sunday morning on our way to church, I asked her to write out the tithe check. She looked at me and said there is not enough money left in the checking account to do that. She said that would be the last time that would happen. From then on the tithe check would be the first one that we would write, and that would no longer be a problem. That's the way it has been for over fifty-six years.

After working at the bank for five years, my boss wanted to relocate and find a banking job in a college town so his children could stay at home and attend college. In January 1967, he left Welch for a new job in Fulton, Missouri. I had already made plans to take an agriculture lending job in Okmulgee, Oklahoma. When my boss knew he was going to leave, he talked to me about staying and running the bank. I told him that I figured I was too young and that the owners would want someone older with more experience. One of the owners called me about the job of running the Welch Bank and asked if I thought I could run the bank as the manager. I told him that I felt I could. My greatest fear of running the bank was a twenty-seven-year-old bank manager trying to give a fifty-year-old farmer advice. I told him I knew they would be putting a lot of faith in me, and I promised him that I would really try not to let the owners down by acting like a "know it all" and causing a lot of the bank's customers to go elsewhere for their banking needs. He said he knew I was young, but that the owners were willing to take that chance of making me the bank manager if I was willing to accept the job. I told him I would accept the position, and that I would surely try not to disappoint him and the board of directors.

When I started managing the bank there were only three employees and a lady that would come in from time to time to help us if we were real busy. The first year that I ran the bank, we made a profit of $17,000.00. The second year the Lord started blessing me and the bank made a profit of over $40,000.00. The owner that hired me was very proud of our accomplishments and asked me how we were able to do it. I shared with him that our bank had not been very progressive, so I asked the ladies that worked for me to take very positive steps to visit with the people that we knew that had banked with us. We invited them back and explained how we could help them and our deposits began to grow and so did our loans. Also, if people couldn't make it in to sign papers on their loan or to open an account, we talked with them by phone and made arrangements to meet them after hours. The best thing we had going for us was the word of mouth advertising that we received from satisfied customers. During those years, I looked for other jobs that I heard about and checked them out. That went on for a period of about ten years, and come to find out, I had a pretty good job right there in Welch, Oklahoma.

Managing the bank provided me the experience of overseeing the construction of a new bank building. Purchasing lots for the location of a new building was an arduous task. The old bank building had served its purpose. I had some bold plans in mind for the future of our bank, and we needed a larger building. The board of directors and I began planning and finally came up with a plan for a 40'x80' colonial style building. I think our budget for the bank was around $300,000.00. The first people I talked with told me that the building we wanted to build could not be done for our budgeted price. I prayed about it, and in a few months the man who took care of our bank vault doors told me he knew of a man, from St. Louis, Missouri, whom he felt could build us the bank building we wanted. I talked to our board of directors and they decided that one of the directors and I should fly to Rolla, Missouri, and talk to the man about constructing a bank building and look at a building he had built there. One of the owners joined us and flew the three of us to Rolla in a small plane. After lunch with the builder, we visited with him and looked at the facility he had built. I asked the men with me what they thought. In 1975, we were able to build the new bank building and in the spring of 1976, we moved into our new 3200 square feet of banking space. I remember we had five employees and the new bank was arranged so that the tellers could also take care of the drive through facility. We have added on to that Welch building two times and it now has over 10,000 square feet.

Sowing and Reaping...a lifestyle

Things were going pretty well and in the early 1980's a real financial down turn occurred in our economy. I experienced a lot of sleepless nights worrying about several sizable cattle loans which seemed to be our greatest risk. I really was not sure, but I thought the bank might fail. I worried about it a great deal and I needed to talk to someone, but who would that be? I finally decided to talk to my Dad. I knew he did not know that much about banking, but I knew that he had a lot of common sense. I will never forget what he said to me. He said, "Charles, you know that I do not know how to run a bank, but if you will ask the Lord to help you and let him be the Chairman of the

Board, I think you will find that everything will work out fine." I took his wise advice and am happy to report that things did work out fine.

After a few years of managing the bank, I came to the conclusion that I wanted to buy a bank, and I talked to the owner that hired me several times about it and he always told me, "You have it pretty good right where you are." I told him I knew I probably would not make a larger salary even if I owned the bank, but that my goal in life was to own one someday. In the fall of 1980, he informed me that the bank's owners were going to sell the bank. I told him I would like the chance to try to purchase it. He told me to figure out what I might be able to do in purchasing the bank. I remember going to Kansas City, Missouri, and talking to a man who worked for the GRA firm that assisted in the purchase of banks through forming a one bank holding company. In 1980 the bank was $11,132,671.02 in size. In 1981, we were able to close on the sale. The size of the bank was $12,306,325.24 and employed four people. The bank owners wanted Arthur Cousatte and me to have the bank, and in all honesty, they really helped us make the purchase. The bank was very small, but the Lord has blessed us beyond what I could ever have imagined. The bank now has total assets of $260,000,000.00, and we have seventy-seven employees at four locations. And we are still growing.

As part of our growth, I wanted to be able to expand the bank's territory and customer base but wasn't sure how to do it. At some point (I don't remember exactly when) I talked to our officers and told them that I would like for them to start attending farm shows, setting up a booth for the bank and talking to people about loans, deposits and other bank services. Our Executive Vice President was in charge of getting this started. We still do farm shows and they have really put us in touch with a lot of people. A few years after we started the farm show gigs, we received an invitation from a bank in Charleston, Missouri, that would show us how to do leasing. Again, our Executive Vice President started our officers out doing leases for commercial business and also for counties, local cities, and towns. We certainly had a learning curve doing the leases, but got better when some of our bank staff went to some conventions and met with several people who helped us improve our lease business. We still have staff going to county commissioners' conventions, setting up our booth, and letting people know we are there to give them a helping hand. At one time, we had leases in all 77 counties of Oklahoma. We also do leases in Arkansas, Texas, and Missouri and for schools in several states. Getting into the leasing business has proven to be very good for our bank.

For several years banks could not branch in Oklahoma. The law was changed and branch banking was allowed. Our first branch opened in Miami on North Main near the Wal-Mart store. Our second expansion was an acquisition of the South Coffeyville, Oklahoma branch from the Regents bank in Nowata, Oklahoma. As we watched Miami's growth and expansion going east, we were able to purchase some property for the purpose of building another branch on Steve Owens Boulevard. Branching has also proven to be very good for our bank.

For several years Welch State Bank has been listed as one of the top performing banks in the United States. I don't look at our standings very often, but in 2009 the bank was ranked 13th in the United States in the Return on Assets area, going from the bank category of $100,000,000.00 to $250,000,000.00. I don't want people to feel like we are bragging so I don't like to say much about these kinds of statistics.

When I reflect over what I have shared with you, I know that I have been a part of a miracle from God. When people talk to me about where I live and they learn that Welch has a population of 650 people and that the bank now has grown to be $260,000,000.00, they are amazed at what has happened. Quite frankly, I am also amazed. All I can say is, "Look what the Lord has done." Arthur and I are not perfect people, but we try to live a Christian life and try to follow the teachings of Jesus. We have been blessed to have a wonderful group of people help make the bank what it is today. I don't feel like we own the bank, but we have been allowed to be God's servants and stewards.

The Miracle of Sowing and Reaping…

Through the years, and especially under Pastor Frizzelle's ministry, God has brought my wife and me to really understand what sowing and reaping is all about. What a blessing it is to give someone a gift and watch them enjoy it. It is truly a blessing and most rewarding to be able to bless someone. We never miss what we give away. My dad was right when he said to make the Lord the Chairman of the Board and everything will be all right.

Thank you, Dad, and to my father in heaven…God… Be the Glory!

CHAPTER 11*
Receiving Your Miracle

If you abide in Me, and My words abide in you, you will ask what you desire, and it shall be done for you.

JOHN 15:7 (NKJV)

Miracles include our response to God and His power (His Word) manifested in our lives and circumstances. In Matthew 14, when Jesus asked Peter to step out of the boat, three things happened. First, Peter started out (moved) when no one else did. Then, he encountered a storm. And finally, most importantly, he saw Jesus remained there (kept his eyes on Jesus). When adversity tries to destroy your faith, Jesus is there. You can count on Him. So, like Peter… keep your eyes on Jesus.

In receiving a miracle, there are two steps to be understood and scripture verses to go with them. These verses are part of the solid foundation of God's Word to stand on when you need a miracle.

- First step: **ASK**

...Yet you do not have because you do not ask.
JAMES 4:26 (NKJV).

Do not fear to step out into faith and ask God to give you what you need. He does not ever want to withhold anything from you. He wants to bless you. It's important to note that we ask and believe, *but God works the miracle.*

- Second Step: **MOVE**

And whatever things you ask in prayer, believing, you will receive.
MATTHEW 21:22 (NKJV)

This is the faith part of the miracle. You have to tell your heart and mind to believe that God is going to do it. This is the area that can be most difficult. I would urge you not to give up. *God's delay is not his denial.*

NEVER GIVE UP!

God is no respector of persons. These faith statements from three biblical examples will help and encourage you to seek your miracle.

2 CHRONICLES 20: concerning Jehoshaphat

vs. 2. "And Jehoshaphat feared, and set himself to seek the Lord, and proclaimed a fast throughout all Judah." **He sought the Lord.**

vs. 12 "O our God, will You not judge them? For we have no power against this great multitude that is coming against us; nor do we know what to do, but our eyes are upon You."
He put his eyes on the Lord

vs. 15 "And he said, 'Listen, all you of Judah and you inhabitants of Jerusalem, and you, King Jehoshaphat! Thus says the LORD to you: 'Do not be afraid nor dismayed because of this great multitude, for the battle is not yours, but God's...' "
God spoke to Him

vs. 17 " 'You will not need to fight in this battle. Position yourselves, stand still and see the salvation of the Lord, who is with you, O Judah and Jerusalem!' Do not fear or be dismayed; tomorrow go out against them, for the Lord is with you."
He positioned himself

vs. 18 "And Jehoshaphat bowed his head with his face to the ground, and all Judah and the inhabitants of Jerusalem bowed before the Lord, worshiping the Lord."
He worshipped God

vs. 19 "Then the Levites of the children of the Kohathites and of the children of the Korahites stood up to praise the Lord God of Israel with voices loud and high."
Worship released God to destroy the enemy

2 KINGS 6: concerning Elisha

vs. 16 "So he answered, 'Do not fear, for those who are with us are more than those who are with them.' "
He knew who was on his side

vs. 17 "And Elisha prayed, and said, 'Lord, I pray, open his eyes that he may see.' Then the Lord opened the eyes of the young man, and he saw. And behold, the mountain was full of horses and chariots of fire all around Elisha."
The Lord opened his servant's eyes

2 KINGS 7: concerning the four lepers

vs. 3 "Now there were four leprous men at the entrance of the gate; and they said to one another, 'Why are we sitting here until we die?' "
They got desperate

vs. 4 "If we say, 'We will enter the city,' the famine is in the city, and we shall die there. And if we sit here, we die also. Now therefore, come, let us surrender to the army of the Syrians. If they keep us alive, we shall live; and if they kill us, we shall only die."
They were willing to move forward at any cost

vs. 5 "And they rose at twilight to go to the camp of the Syrians; and when they had come to the outskirts of the Syrian camp, to their surprise no one was there."
God used their faith to move forward to win a victory

vs. 8 "And when these lepers came to the outskirts of the camp, they went into one tent and ate and drank, and carried from it silver and gold and clothing, and went and hid them; then they came back and entered another tent, and carried some from there also, and went and hid it."
They received the blessing

vs. 9 "Then they said to one another, 'We are not doing right. This day is a day of good news, and we remain silent. If we wait until morning light, some punishment will come upon us.

Now therefore, come, let us go and tell the king's household.' "
They shared the blessing

In summary:

- **Get your eyes on God**
- **Position yourself**
- **Ask God to open your eyes**
- **Obey**
- **Move forward to your miracle**

As we pray for... believe for...and expect miracles... it is essential to recognize and to know the greatest miracle we receive is salvation. Every time we pray and ask for a miracle, and believe for one, we must rest in the wisdom and power of God for His answer. It's not faith in our faith, but faith in God, who is the miracle worker. Hebrews Chapter 11 describes miracles that happen, and yet some did not seem to receive what they prayed and hoped for in this life. Their greatest miracle was making heaven. I've seen miracles happen and I've seen times the miracle prayed and hoped for did not happen in this life...but we keep praying, asking and believing for miracles as we trust Jesus to do the God part and we do our part...we keep our eyes on Him.

I'm believing and knowing miracles will continue to happen in our lives, as well as those in our church family and throughout the kingdom of God. I'm believing, knowing, and expecting miracles to continue...and continue......and continue...... And the testimonies of those miracles will continue on......and on......and on.........

May you be blessed and walk in God's best. Keep trusting and keep getting out of your boat...keep your eyes on Jesus...keep moving and walking on the water.

Pastor Raymond Frizzelle

God is on a mission to bring miracles in your life, so **GET READY!**
The very trial you are experiencing has a miracle wrapped and hidden
in it. God will not waste your pain or experiences. He uses all of it to
bring about growth and change in us. He desires to have a relationship with each of us. Seek Him and He will be found. I'm believing
with you that in your life MIRACLES can happen…and that they will
happen.

ABOUT THE AUTHOR

Raymond Frizzelle is an ordained minister with the Assemblies of God and has devoted his life to kingdom work. Until he draws his last breath, he will pray for one more soul to be added to the kingdom of God and witness one more miracle. He and his wife, Cynthia, were born and raised in the Dallas-Ft. Worth metropolitan area and continue, together, in ministry.

Frizzelle attended Christ for the Nations Bible School and has been involved in many areas of ministry all of his career. Especially notable is years of missionary work in addition to his pastoral assignments in the churches he has served. He preached his first sermon in 1970 on "Loving People into the Kingdom." LOVE, GRACE and MIRACLES are the soul of the Frizzelles' ministry.

He currently serves as Presbyter of Oklahoma District Assemblies of God section 1 and is Senior Pastor at Miami First Assembly of God Church, Miami, OK.

Find our website at:
https://www.miamifirstag.org/

Find us on Facebook at:
Miami First Assembly of God (Miami, OK)

Email Pastor at:
raymond@miamifirstag.org

walkingonthewaterbook@gmail.com